IDENTITY PROTECTION:
COPYRIGHT, RIGHT OF PUBLICITY, AND THE ARTIST'S NEGATIVE VOICE

Jeff Klein

A Thesis

Submitted to the Graduate College of Bowling Green
State University in partial fulfillment of
the requirements for the degree of

MASTER OF MUSIC

May 2014

Committee:

Katherine Meizel, Advisor

Jeremy Wallach

Kara Attrep

ABSTRACT

Katherine Meizel, Advisor

What do you value most about your voice?

As ethnomusicological studies of the voice expand, so must our understanding of what voice even means. Voice must entail more than just a sonic phenomenon, but must also relate to ideology, to our very identity, even. This thesis will fuse ethnomusicological and legal perspectives to explore how American and, to a lesser extent, international copyright law and other legal mechanisms protect more than just a musician's economic interest, but also his very identity. I will explore the right of publicity and the concept of moral rights and how they relate to voice and identity. The right of publicity is a musician's right to protect his identity as well as his copyrighted works while moral rights is the right of a musician to prevent certain uses of his work even when he has assigned the copyright of that work to another. This thesis will suggest a theoretical framework for investigating the voice as an intangible legal marker of identity.

This thesis will examine where copyright law protects identity and where it falls short and how the right of publicity fills in the gaps to provide comprehensive protection for a musician's voice in the broadest sense. It will provide a background on the scope of copyright law, as well as how it has historically developed to protect more than just work-product, but also the musician's very identity. It will then explore the right of publicity and moral rights and how those ideas fit into the general legal scheme of copyright protection. I will accomplish this through interviews with musicians, as well as explorations of current scholarly work on identity, copyright, voice, the right of publicity, and moral rights. I will also explore important legal cases and relevant statutes in these areas, such as *Tom Waits v. Frito-Lay*, *Bette Midler v. Ford Motor Company* and the Copyright Act of 1976. These explorations can help us understand how musicians can protect their identity by protecting their ideological, as well as their physical, voices.

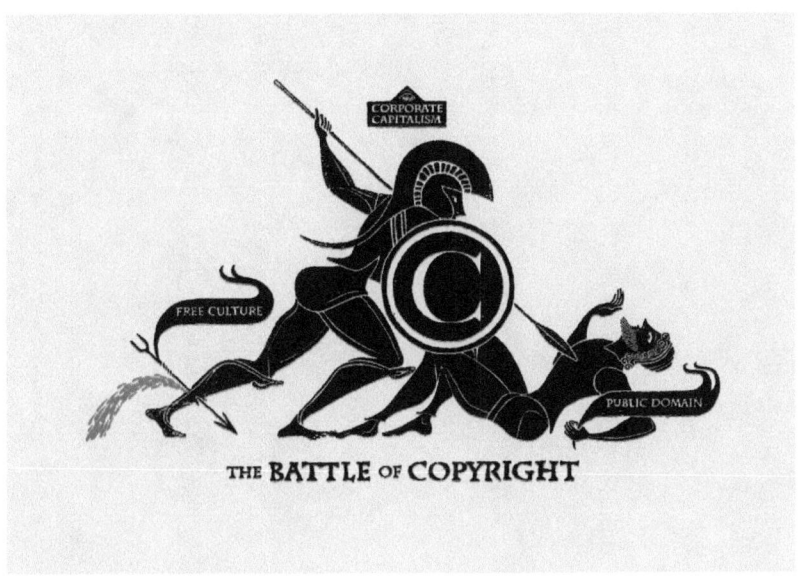

This thesis is dedicated to Julie for just being amazing.

ACKNOWLEDGMENTS

I would like to acknowledge the faculty of the College of Musical Arts at Bowling Green State University and, in particular, my thesis committee, Drs. Katherine Meizel, Kara Attrep, and Jeremy Wallach, for their support throughout my long journey. I would particularly like to acknowledge Dr. David Harnish who sparked my interest in ethnomusicology, an interest that would become nothing short of a transformative journey that would open my mind and change my life in ways I never could have dreamed.

TABLE OF CONTENTS

INTRODUCTION

What defines a musician?

It is difficult enough to define any human being, but musicians, and other celebrities, are especially difficult because of the unique place they hold in society. Musicians spend tremendous amounts of time and money to create an identity to present to their fans. Their fans, in turn, base their opinions about those musicians upon those portrayed identities.

In this thesis, I will explore identity from the standpoint of musicians, consider the influences that shape and inform their identity creation and perpetuation, and explore the ways in which musicians can protect their identities from exploitation. I accomplish this by studying identity and how the legal system, both at home and abroad, functions to protect identity for musicians. This is most salient when a third party co-opts a musician's identity in some way that impugns that musician's reputation or belief system, usually by using that identity in advertising. This belief system may not only shape that musician's identity, but also lends to their credibility and, therefore, their influence amongst their fan base. Reputation, then, becomes not only a primary ethical concern for musicians, but also a significant economic one.

As I began my fieldwork for this project, a couple of things surprised me. My initial plan was to interview Bette Midler, Tom Waits, and other celebrity musicians who were associated with product endorsement. I reached out to the representatives of dozens of such musicians from the ones I just noted to Taylor Swift, Demi Lovato, Ingrid Michaelson, CeeLo Green, and others. When I heard back from a total of three of them, all denials, I was forced to lower my sights a bit and approach local and regional musicians instead.

I interviewed seven musicians, six of whom were primarily operating on the creative side of the spectrum and one of whom worked both as a musician and as a producer. Sarah is a jazz vocalist who has released two albums and has composed multiple songs protected by copyright. Ben is a jazz clarinetist and big band leader who has released several recordings under a smaller jazz-based label. Tom is also a big band leader who has released several albums, but whose work has been used in multiple regional television commercials. Matt is a folk rock guitarist and singer who has recorded albums both with his band and as a solo artist and has also been featured in multiple regional commercials. Norah is also a jazz vocalist who has recorded one album with a small, local label, but has appeared on other albums as a background vocalist. Will is a jazz guitarist and vocalist who has recorded his own albums, but has also worked for record labels as a producer. Finally, Steve is the front man for a rock band signed to a major label that has released several albums containing original music. One of their songs is currently the theme of a successful television series on a major cable network. Each of these informants has had different types of exposure to record companies on multiple levels, providing a reasonably broad range of perspectives.

Going into these interviews, I expected my informants to have given the concepts I was asking about, such as identity and voice, very little thought, but to know quite a bit about copyright law, which is, after all, their bread and butter. I was surprised, though, at how considered and developed some of their ideas were on the theoretical concepts, but also with how little some of them knew about copyright law.

This helped reinforce the importance of fieldwork to me. There is no reason I couldn't have done this project without fieldwork. Concrete examples certainly help to reinforce ideas by grounding them in the real world, but this thesis had some concrete examples built in, so I believe the project still would have been meaningful without fieldwork. What that type of approach lacks, though, is dialogue.

The dialogues I had with my informants helped me to understand the musician's perspective in a more nuanced way than what I could get from the work of others. Of course, when you rely upon someone else's work, you're limited to the questions they thought to ask and their perspectives. Having the freedom to explore my own ideas in my own way was far more meaningful to me in terms of understanding my object. In fact, my fieldwork led directly to some of the most important ideas in this thesis.

I chose to keep my informants' identities confidential. While I did not ask all of the informants whether they wanted to remain anonymous, during an interview, one of the informants had expressed a concern regarding disclosing his identity. He was a musician, but also worked in management on the production side of the business. I interviewed him at the same time as another of my informants and they both expressed concern that if record companies found out about their interviews and didn't like what they said, it would negatively impact their professional lives. Honestly, I don't know whether those concerns were founded or just mild paranoia, but they seemed legitimate enough to support my decision to keep all of the informants' identities confidential. After all, none of my informants were big names who might be able to stand up to a record company and I did not want to risk any potential adverse professional repercussions for them, so it seemed like the safe route. Especially on an issue as divisive between musicians and record companies as copyright. If an informant wanted to take a public stand, that would have been one thing. If not, the risk seemed real enough for me to be cautious and I kept their identities secret.

The second thing that surprised me was how incomplete my theory was going into my fieldwork. I was working with the negative voice, a theory I had previously developed, so first, I had to justify where that theory came from and why it was different from what was out there already. After all, Mladen Dolar, for example, did talk about the power of silence, so it's not as if this was completely new territory. (Dolar 2006) My theories were different from what Dolar was describing, though. Dolar was speaking of the phenomenon of aural silence rather than ideological silence. In fact, most of the existing scholarly work on silence seemed to focus on the aural aspect rather than the ideological.

It occurred to me that developing a way of theorizing the ideological voice in a way that was similar to theorizing the aural voice was the key. There are three ways to consider the aural voice. When considering the aural voice, you may consider the actual sound, the meaning of the sound, and the mechanisms that produce the sound. You can use a similar framework for the ideological voice. You can consider the action that someone takes, the ideological position that action represents, and the mechanism that enables that action. That is the additional step I have taken with my formulation of the ideological voice that was informed by my fieldwork.

Moving on to copyright law, in reading many of the works I studied for this thesis, there was a general cynicism about copyright law and its usefulness to musicians. Indeed, there seemed to be quite a vocal outcry against copyright law as protecting record companies and not musicians, and not without good reason. In fact, Matt Stahl recently published a book on that very topic where he examined the power imbalance between record companies and musicians. (Stahl 2012)

Copyright law was originally developed to promote creativity. Today, with protection often lasting over 100 years and rights generally being assigned to record companies so that the creators aren't being protected anyway, it is hard to consider how copyright law promotes creativity. Kembrew McLeod explores copyright in general and recognizes that record companies wield a powerful tool of suppression. He contends that, "when companies try to use intellectual-property law to censor speech they don't like, they are abusing the reason why these exist in the first place." (McLeod 2005, 8) McLeod takes a very extreme position, but not an inaccurate one.

In light of this, it was important to explore the ways musicians do have control over their economic success. If it does not come from copyright royalties, where does it come from? And how can musicians control their financial success? I spent a great deal of time considering those questions and, as it turned out, those answers became the theme that would tie all of the separate parts of this thesis together.

I began with the general idea that I would be studying the ways in which the law acted to protect identity. In the end, though, everything comes down to money or power and I realized it was these themes that would become central to my thesis. While identity does not, in and of itself, carry a tangible value, it is still highly valuable. In fact, it is the ability to cultivate this identity that is central to the only leverage that a musician really has over a major record company. They generally assign their copyrights to the company, so copyright law has no real functional value to musician. But fame provides musicians with artistic freedom, financial rewards, and leverage over record companies. These financial rewards come from advances from record companies, concert tours, merchandising, advertising, and numerous other sources. Record sales are merely a reflection of a musician's fame and a representation of the acceptance of their identities. So, like it or not, record sales are largely driven by identity. If there is any doubt, just ask Milli Vanilli.

Perhaps this seems like a relatively insignificant thing, but when we consider the power that musicians have over their fans, it is easy to see why voice and identity studies are so important in music. Musicians are a cultural phenomenon and their identities, which are tied into and often manifested in their voice, are what shape that phenomenon. The more complete and nuanced our understanding of musicians, their identities and voice, how they are created, and how they influence public perception and cultural capital, the better able we are to incorporate this understanding into a broader conceptual framework to understand cultural forces and change in general.

It is in this light that I will discuss how identity relates to the legal system, specifically copyright law, in a meaningful way to protect musicians. This is not only important because of the consequences of identity, but also because of the significance of the legal system to musicians and ethnomusicologists. In 1992, Anthony Seeger called for ethnomusicologists to engage in studies of the legal system "not because it represents yet one more example of ingenuity for complexification found in *homo sapiens*, but because the daily exercise of our profession takes place within contexts partly defined by it." (Seeger 1992, 345). Seeger was primarily theorizing in the context of field recordings and the relationship between subject and object, but it also benefits us to have a more nuanced understanding of the multifaceted ways in which the legal system interacts with music as a process, music as a product, and music as it relates to musicians and their identity.[1]

---

[1] As an attorney and an ethnomusicologist I have observed a dramatic difference in the way those two groups conceive of the legal system. Ethnomusicologists often consider the judiciary as a capitalist tool of oppression while legal practitioners recognize that this is not how the legal system actually functions. This is a topic worth exploring further, but I opted not to open that can of worms here in the interest of keeping my focus on my particular object.

How we define copyright impacts what it protects by simultaneously providing clarity and also imposing the boundaries that limit its protection. These limitations are a central focus of this thesis. By breaking free of labels and broadening our gaze to understand copyright within a bigger picture, we can begin to see how natural it is to conceive of copyright as a means of protecting identity. In their 2004 book about copyright, Simon Frith and Lee Marshall suggest that "it is particularly important to understand copyright in terms that are not simply derived from rights owners' property claims but also consider the broader effects of copyright on creativity and the social circulation of ideas." (Frith and Marshall 2004, 5)

In this light, in the second chapter I will explore the factual and philosophical history and development of copyright law. I will trace this development beginning with the Statute of Anne in England in the late nineteenth century and follow it internationally and through America to highlight where its growth followed similar developmental paths in both arenas and where it has diverged. I will also discuss how both foreign and domestic copyright law is once again converging. This is a necessary first step to understanding the interests copyright law protects and those that it does not so that it becomes possible to better understand the way the law has expanded to protect new rights and has evolved to fill gaps in copyright protection.

The third chapter explores the right of publicity, a judicially created creature of intellectual property law designed to protect intangible rights not contemplated by copyright law. I will demonstrate, through case law, how the right of publicity has evolved through three stages of development from initially protecting only visual images and representations of celebrities to ultimately protecting their identity and ideologies, as well. This is relevant because it also tracks how our conceptions of the law can change over time and it serves as a benchmark for how copyright law has been developing in the courts. I, therefore, draw parallels between copyright and the right of publicity. This leads directly into my discussions of moral rights in the following chapter.

In the fourth chapter, I will introduce the moral rights doctrine, a concept that serves as the cornerstone for my arguments that copyright law, in its various forms, can protect identity. The moral rights doctrine is a legislative creature that protects the use of an artist's product (music or visual art, for example) from uses that conflict with the artist's morals or ideology. This doctrine is relatively common in international copyright law and has been adopted by the Berne Convention, an organization providing a legal framework for international copyright protection and enforcement, but has not yet been applied to music in America. In this chapter, I will argue that the tide has begun rising toward providing this protection to music in America and that the legislative protection of music by the moral rights doctrine is not just a possibility, but an inevitability.

In the fifth chapter, I will introduce the concepts of the positive and negative voices and how they interact to represent a musician's identity. The positive voice consists of affirmative actions that represent a musician's identity. The negative voice can be simply thought of as the practice of speaking without saying anything at all. Often, the things we do not say are as telling as the things we do say. The negative voice is a musician's intentional use of that concept in order to establish an ideology. By way of example, Tom Waits has a long-standing disdain for musicians who align themselves with advertisers and products. He demonstrates this ideology not just through his words, but also through his lack of action in choosing not to endorse any products or have his name associated with any commercial ventures. This is something his fans have come to expect from him and it has become an important and intentional part of his reputation and credibility. Any deviation from this norm would have a profound impact on his image and that credibility amongst his fans. By choosing not to speak in favor of any specific products, Tom Waits has spoken rather clearly on his opinion of those products and their commercialization.

In the sixth chapter, I will summarize the conceptual framework I established in the first five chapters to draw all of these threads together and weave them into an argument that the fact that copyright and intellectual property law work together to protect both work product and identity, voice, and ideology is not just a development, but an evolutionary mandate. In this way, the legal system is protecting both creations of the creative mind and the identity of those who create them. I go further than just that, though, by also considering whether copyright law as it exists is effective at providing the protections it is intended to provide and whom it actually protects. In a sense, this chapter focuses a very critical eye upon copyright law as it currently exists in America, but also explore why it has developed the way it has and suggest that this developmental path was not just necessary, but also beneficial for the music industry and the promotion of creativity in general. I will also consider some of the problems that technology presents for modern copyright holders and the ways in which technology might inform the development of copyright law going forward.

Musicians are making inroads at eroding the still substantial power of record companies. Radiohead is the most obvious example of a band that has chosen to avoid record companies entirely, but other smaller musicians are helping cultivate a DIY industry that enables musicians to retain rights in their music while, as always, utilizing their identities as a powerful economic driver. Filking[2] would be just one example of a genre that benefits from this type of business model. This industry includes crowdsourcing-type companies that will handle marketing for

---

[2] Folk music based upon a fandom such as Harry Potter or Firefly.

musicians for a fee while allowing musicians to retain control over their intellectual property rights. The more musicians who choose this route, the greater the collective power of these companies will be. It's kind of like the print-on-demand self-publishing industry for writers.

So what does all this mean in the long run? These ideas, my discursive theory of comparing the aural and ideological voice, and my positive/negative formulation of ideological voice are powerful analytical tools. Aside from that, an explicit statement of how identity functions as an economic tool and a marker of power for musicians with respect to record companies is useful. Voice studies are a growing area in ethnomusicology and, as that area expands, we have come to better understand what a complicated word "voice" is. This thesis, then, uses a fine paintbrush to add some detail to an already expansive and complex canvas.

CHAPTER I
EXPLORING IDENTITY AND THE SELF

The logical starting point for my study is the foundational concept of identity itself. Identity has been theorized in many contexts and may mean very different things dependant upon that context. As it relates to this project, identity works together with voice, each informing the other, to create a product, of sorts. Thinking of identity as a product is helpful in theorizing it with respect to copyright law because current discourse on copyright generally focuses on protection of a product. This is not universal, of course. Academics have also focused on different formulations of rights in order to consider the ways in which the law can protect those rights.

One example is the treatise *Music & Cultural Rights*, edited by Andrew Weintraub and Bell Yung. This book contains chapters written on numerous issues relating to cultural rights around the world, Weintraub defining the concept of "cultural rights" in his introduction as "proprietary and proprietary-related assertions based on cultural grounds," (Weintraub 2009, 1) and concludes with a chapter addressing the need for a cross-cultural legal framework. Some examples of cultural rights would include representations of culture through music, how government policies affect those representations, and the moral and ethical implications of those policies. This aspect of law in music is a "consideration of what happens when 'culture' takes on new and varied forms of materiality." (Myers 2004, 6) While this is a significant concern, it does fall outside the scope of this study. It bears mentioning, though, because it serves to illustrate the ways in which the law is conceived of and theorized to protect issues outside of music as a product or process.

The Individual and the Collective: Defining Identity

Identity is a difficult concept to define and theorize, but all the more so when applied to musicians. Musicians hold a unique place in society. Whether we choose to acknowledge it or not, musicians hold a tremendous amount of power over their fans and over shaping society in general.[3] While this influence is most noticeable when we are talking about celebrity musicians, that is not to say that local or regional musicians do not hold sway over their fan base. As I learned from my informants, they have an active fan base and are aware of the esteem in which they are held. In a sense, their influence over their fans is more direct than that of celebrity musicians because they have a more active engagement with those fans. This power is inextricably tied to identity: the musician's, the fans', members of society at large, and, to be certain, the infinite number of combinations that exist between each of those factors. Fans feel a strong connection with the object of their interest and the musicians have a unique opportunity to capitalize upon that interest. This capitalization can be either artistic or economic, but is most often both.

This begs the question, then, of why musicians hold such an elevated status in our society. Celebrities, in general, are idolized in our society, but musicians are held in even higher esteem… and disdain. Even outside of a musical context, it is not uncommon to hear someone who is wildly popular or respected in a certain social sphere to be referred to as a "rock star." This moniker generally has a positive association, but real "rock stars" have their fair share of negative associations, too. The holy trinity of unhealthy lifestyle is sex, drugs, and rock and roll

---

[3] Further research focusing on celebrities may be found in the journal *Celebrity Studies*.

and they are almost inextricably linked in popular culture. Musicians become a locus for negotiating power relations and identity politics, establishing collective identity, driving commercialism, and defining cultural groupings. It is this complex web that I would like to unravel a bit.

The driving force behind this complex dynamic is not an easy one to identify and cannot be reduced to some neat and tidy binary or defined in a single sentence. There is the Western social elevation of musical talent that marks the musician as someone special and, in some respects, above non-musicians. (Blacking 1973) There is the powerful marketing arm of record companies, whose very profitability and existence capitalizes on and relies upon this elevation. There is the wealth and extravagant lifestyle that so many rock stars display, nay flaunt, to the public that separates the "haves" from the "have-nots" and the entitled from the envious. And there is the need to perpetuate this lifestyle and these perceptions in order to maintain the lifestyle and feed the addiction to money, fame, and power that many rock stars develop as a result of the intoxicating power of this dynamic.

Of course, it would be cynical to simply focus on the power and corruption inherent in this construction of celebrity. There are also positive uses of this power and many musicians utilize their cultural cache in order to effectuate positive change and endeavor to improve the societies in which they exist. Bono from U2 and Sting immediately come to mind, but there are countless other examples, as well. In a sense, the entire American folk music movement of the 1960s was an attempt to effectuate positive social change through music. These factors are equally involved in the shaping of, and informed by, identity and the use of voice. It is these concepts around which the universe of the phenomenon of the rock star revolves.

Individual Identity

Thomas Turino states that individual identity "involves the *partial* selection of habits and attributes used to represent oneself to oneself and others and to others by oneself and by others." (Turino 2008, 95) He further explains that "our bodies and the social environment operate in dialectical ways throughout a lifetime to shape habits of thought and practice." (100) While musicians are certainly not the only factor operating within Turino's "social environment" to influence identity, they are undeniably influential. A dialogue requires the exchange of information in both directions, though, and it is the society with which musicians interact that frames this dialogue and its reciprocal effects. This dialogue is also temporal. Psychologists Lauren Duncan and Abigail Stewart have contextualized this temporality when discussing collective identity. They explained that "some individuals feel a deep connection to their time and place in history... that they are products of large social events and processes and that events in their personal lives are understood best by reference to social forces and movements." (Duncan and Stewart 2007, 143) I would add that music and, by extension, the musicians that music is associated with play a crucial role in that temporality.

Identity is a much more troubling concept than Turino's construction, as convoluted as it is, lets on. Even within that construction, which I am actually quite comfortable with, there are countless implied layers, subtleties, and nuances. There are several different types of identity that we can identify. For example, context plays a significant role in the perception of identity. People I interact with in a professional environment are likely to see a different facet of my identity than people I interact with socially. A significant other is privy to a side of me that nobody else is. Ron Scollon discusses the notion that there are multiple manifestations of identity in his study of the Chinese concept of Face as the "difference between "*miànzi* and *liân*, between an "outer" or social face and an "inner" or personal character face." (Scollon 1995, 14) There are, of course, more than just two such manifestations, but a nearly infinite number dependent upon context. We can consider these different contexts facets of a greater whole, but each no less important to identity construction than the others. This then begs the question of whether there is a *true* identity as opposed to perceived identity. If there were such a thing as a true identity, then it would have to be objective and verifiable. Even if there is such a thing, we must be cognizant of the fact that this objective identity most certainly differs from our own perceived identity of self, with the self being "a sense of who and what we are." (Kleine, Kleine, and Kernan 1993, 209) Self, then, is necessarily subjective and rarely a reflection of who and what we really are. Nobody is a more effective con artist of the self than the self.

However, one of the reasons identity is difficult to conceptualize in terms of real and perceived is the fact that it is self-validating. We might perceive ourselves in a way that is counter to reality, but the very act of forming that perception incorporates it into our identity in some way, thereby making it real. In a sense, it is impossible to portray facets of identity that are not real because they become real the moment they are presented. In fact, the very act of forming a "false" identity is, in a sense, its own facet of individual identity.

Identity, then, can be parsed out in multiple ways. There is true, objective identity (more of a concept than a reality) and there is perceived identity, which can then be divided into our own perceived identity, which is tied into our sense of self, and our identity as perceived by others, which can then be divided into multiple formations dependent upon context. In reality, the only true identity we have is the one that is comprised of all of those constructs, in their infinite numbers, variations, complexities, and nuances, and how they interact with and inform each other.

As it relates to my fieldwork, my informants had many different ideas about identity, each focusing on something different, yet all similar in some way. One common thread between them was that they all acknowledged that identity reflects a conscious decision of the musician and, as Sarah put it, "is the largest part of their act and is crucial to their success." However, she also told me that, "I think my private life is well represented in my public work. I've always found it too much work to bother creating a persona on stage so I think both my musical and personal identities are very closely related." (Interview, November 10, 2012) This suggests an organicism and realness of her public identity that grows out of her private identity.

Tom told me that he has, "difficulty fabricating and marketing a specific brand or image so I rely on my body of work to create my public image." (Interview, December 19, 2012) The connection he made between his identity and his work as almost being one in the same was interesting, but I think lacking in an important sense. The important question being *how* his work is reflective of his identity and why he made the choice of unifying his public identity with that reflected in his work in the first place. It is also worth asking whether it is possible for your work *not* to reflect your identity in some meaningful way.

This type of sincerity was reflected by Ben, who noted that he thinks, "Identity is purely being as 'real' as you can be… I try to just be myself… people respond to sincerity." He followed this statement up, though, with a general statement about his own public and private personas by telling me that he is, "a bit more reserved off stage. Not comfortable in social situations… I am much more outgoing on stage." (Interview, December 17, 2012) This suggests an artificiality of identity, in a sense, despite his claim to sincerity. Artificiality was reflected much more explicitly in my discussion with another informant who had a different approach to identity and noted the importance of focusing on good production value because, "real life is a lot messier and more uncertain for me." This is a stark contrast to the first two informants because this explicitly acknowledges an intentional artificiality of individual public identity that implicitly marks a difference between the two.

The thing that was common between all of my informants, though, was the fact that all were conscious of the existence of an identity as a musician and the fact that they had to consider and make decisions regarding the nature of that identity. Even where my informants chose to present an identity to their fans that was consonant with what they perceived as their non-public identities, there is still an artificiality about their public identities because of the fact that it was shaped and is the result of a conscious and considered decision.

If individual identity is as boundless a concept as I have suggested in this formation, how can we possibly hope to study it in any meaningful way? In a sense, it is impossible. In another sense, though, we can endeavor to identify and acknowledge as many of these identities as possible and use them to inform our treatment of our research object. Each individual study then goes to inform discourse on that, and related, objects and helps shape perception of those objects. It is through the development of this complex discursive web that our understanding of the world around us becomes more nuanced and meaningful.

Collective Identity

To this point, I have just discussed individual identity, but there is another construction of identity that also creates strands within our complex conceptual web. Collective identity is a social construct that "addresses the 'we-ness' of a group, stressing the similarities or shared attributes around which group members coalesce." (Cerulo 1997, 386) Collective identity, of course, is a very complex notion because it relies upon complex interactions within a collective. In collective identity, "identities emerge and movements ensue because collectives consciously coordinate action; group members consciously develop offenses and defenses, consciously insulate, differentiate, and mark, cooperate and compete, persuade and coerce." (393) We might also add the word "unconsciously" to that definition because subconscious actions are also very real influences on collective identity.

These collective identities can also be thought of as what Turino refers to as cultural or identity cohorts. "*Cultural cohort* or *identity cohort* [refers] to social groupings that form along the lines of specific constellations of shared habit based in similarities of *parts* of the self." (Turino 2008, 111) Members of cultural cohorts are "constantly being identified by others because of attributes and deep-seated habits operating below their own focal awareness but clearly noticeable to others." (102) As ethnomusicologist Katherine Meizel explains, "culture in the United States is created in the continuous negotiation and renegotiation of these identities – of personal, community, and national identities, informed by ideas about race and ethnicity, religion, place, gender, and what it means to be American." (Meizel 2011b, 3)

Because this type of identity relies upon social interaction, we might also think of it as social identity, or "the multifaceted labels by which (a collective member's) Me is recognized by themselves and members of society." (Kleine, Kleine, and Kernan 1993, 212) These collectives, or cohorts, then operate together to influence culture. As Meizel explains, "popular music is a key source of these identity markers, which help to shape understandings of Americanness." (Meizel 2011b, 3) Musicians play a key role in this process because they are often the focal point of cultural cohorts or, more accurately, elevated above the cultural cohort as a whole as if on a pedestal. These cohort leaders, if you will, are then in a unique position to shape social identity, which then trickles down to affect individual identity, which then informs perceived identity. A sort of trickle-down economics of identity.

This entire discussion revolves around the idea of identity politics. Identity politics is not an easy concept to define, but one formulation of it is "the activism engaged in by status-based social movements." (Bernstein 2005, 48) Stated more succinctly, identity politics and, to be certain, identity in general, are nothing more than negotiations of power and influence. Musicians, in a sense, are a product that participates in this negotiation because they are a focal point of certain cultural cohorts that shape identity and "the salience or importance of an identity to people drives them to enact its behavior, using identity-associated products." (Kleine, Kleine, and Kernan 1993, 210) These negotiations are ultimately effectuated through the use of voice.

Theorizing the Voice in the Context of Identity

On the surface, the voice is the product of the physical apparatuses that produce sound and shape that sound into a representation of thought. The thing that separates this idea of voice from mere sound is the conveyance of meaning. However, sounds that would not be contemplated by this formation of voice do carry meaning. A cough or sneeze, for example, might carry the meaning of illness or allergy. However, it is important to have some method by which to separate physical sound from voice or one term swallows up the other and there is no need for either.

Traditional voice studies generally theorize voice in its relation to speech, but "a comprehensive vision (of voice) demands a concept that transcends individual fields of study, and encompasses the dizzying array of aesthetic, philosophical, linguistic, acoustic, cognitive, and sociopolitical factors that impact how we produce and hear voices." (Meizel 2011a, 1) This sentiment is echoed by Cavarero when she states that "the original aspect of vocality, as a new object of study, therefore concerns an analysis of voice that avoids the traditional privileging of its relationship with language." (Cavarero 2005, 12) Under this fairly new approach to voice and vocality, there is more to a voice than simply a sonic phenomenon. Simon Frith stated that "the voice… is as important for the way we listen as for the way we interpret what we hear." (Frith 1996, 192) I take that to mean that the voice is not only what is said, but also what is communicated. Adriana Cavarero confirms this when she explains that "before making itself speech, the voice is an invocation that is addressed to the other." (Cavarero 2005, 169).

Roland Barthes' famous definition of the "grain" of the voice is that "the 'grain' is the body in the voice as it sings, the hand as it writes, the limb as it performs." (Barthes 1977, 188) This formulation seems to allow for the non-verbal voice, but can it also be applied to an idea? He goes further to state that our culture "wants art, wants music, provided they be clear, that they 'translate' an emotion and represent a signified." (185) People search for the meaning in things that they consume, so while they are hearing the sonic sensation of a physical voice, what they are searching for is a hermeneutic meaning behind those sounds. I believe that the underlying search for meaning permits the voice, and consequently the grain of the voice, to refer to identity in addition to sound. This, then, would be our ideological voice, or the aspect of voice that reflects our identity, in all of its complexities.

Voice also becomes a marker for sincerity and credibility. Frith notes that "we use the voice, that is, not just to assess a person, but also, even more systematically, to assess that person's sincerity: the voice and how it is used (as well as words and how they are used) become a measure of someone's truthfulness." (Frith 1996, 197) Voice, then, is a key marker in the construction of individual and collective identity, as well as a key component of the commercial, commodified product that musicians create as a facet of their identities. Communication scholars Carol Padden and Tom Humphries, in considering the use of voice in deaf culture, posited that "voice can usefully be thought of as a technology: it is not merely a biological quality or a medium of expression, but an entity to be cultivated, managed, and most recently, converted into a commercial commodity." (Padden and Humphries 2006, 101)

Of course, viewing voice as a technology dehumanizes the voice. Composer Miriama Young addressed this phenomenon when she discussed "the separation of the voice from the body from which it originally emanated – the emergence of the *disembodied voice.*" (Young 2006, 83) She discussed the disembodied, or acousmatic, voice in reference to the development of recording technology. The phonograph allowed people to hear the voice without seeing the body, a phenomenon we are now completely accustomed to, but which was probably quite shocking at its inception. As a result of phonographic recording equipment, "the voice became free-floating, no longer rooted in a particular body, or to a specific locale." (83-84) Another form of the disembodied voice is found on the printed page and reflected in what we think of as the "writer's voice." Writer Alvarez describes that as "the vehicle by which a writer expresses his aliveness." (Alvarez 2004, 23) This type of formulation of voice becomes very important in identity studies because it allows us the conceptual freedom to apply the concept of voice to more than just the sonic phenomenon. As a result, voice is, in fact, one of the most powerful influences on negotiations of power, identity politics, creating cultural or identity cohorts, and shaping individual and collective identity.

When I interviewed my informants, I wanted to get a sense of what they thought of when I mentioned the term "voice." I think that I expected all of them, as vocalists, to focus on the physical production of sound, but I was somewhat surprised by their answers. They ran the gamut from covering both the physical and ideological voice by acknowledging that voice, "could literally mean the sound I produce with my mouth when I speak or sing, or it could mean the character behind that sound: the soul, the phrasing, the humor, or the emotion" to voice being a reflection of musical style as "the lyrical and/or musical style that a certain artist has developed" to the explicit acknowledgement of this ideological voice where voice can be, "your personal opinion concerning something." The thing that each of these statements about voice had in common is that each of them contemplated something other than merely the physical production of sound. I couldn't help but wonder, though, whether those responses were preexisting ideas or whether knowing that they were being interviewed for an academic paper caused my informants to think about this idea in a way that they never had before. One thing that was consistent amongst each of my informants is that they all associated voice with identity or ideology.

More than just a single concept susceptible to simple definition, identity ends up being a very complex web of different concepts, theories, actions, beliefs, and perceptions that define the different ways we see ourselves and the different ways others perceive us. Individual and collective identity both operate in a dialectical manner through voice to inform each other and influence their growth in ways that can be harnessed and used for pecuniary gain. This is the phenomenon that record companies rely upon to drive record sales and provide them with their profits and power over musicians. It is also the phenomenon that the musician can turn to his financial advantage in order to use certain aspects of his identity to perpetuate the mystique of his perceived identity and enjoy the power, money, and fame that comes with the elevated social position of the "rock star" and the influence they have on their cultural cohorts and society at large.

CHAPTER II
THE HISTORIC DEVELOPMENT OF COPYRIGHT LAW

Having explored the complexities of identity and the interactions between identity and

the voice, I turn my attention from the conceptual to the more concrete and consider the

development of copyright law. This discussion is more one of history than theory, but it is

important to understand where copyright law comes from and how it has developed in order to

understand both where it currently stands and what it truly protects and to consider the ways in

which it might develop in the future. As musicians become foci of cultural collectives, the

musician and the collective become mutually dependent in an almost dysfunctional way, each

informing and relying upon the other. Creatures of their own making, musicians often find their

identity is a more valuable commodity than their music. Identity then, as with any product or

commodity, can be exploited, attacked, and damaged, both from outside and within. As the

commercial product of the musician's music is informed by the musician's identity, identity

becomes as important as the physical work product. As such, what role does the law have in

protecting a musician's interest in his identity and how has the law responded to the need for

such protections?

I begin, though, with a question. What do you think of when someone mentions the word

"copyright?"

Chances are pretty good that you think of either piracy or copyright infringement,[4] and

with good reason. Those are the two most prevalent concerns in copyright law, both for

---

[4] By copyright infringement, I mean one artist using another artist's work product without
compensation and claiming it as their own.

musicians and for the recording industry in general. Piracy, as a concept that deals with the relationship between a copyright holder and consumers, is a hotly contested issue, both from an economic standpoint as represented by the music industry's efforts to curb the practice and from an academic perspective. Many scholars (and record industry executives) believe that "piracy is the greatest threat facing the music industry worldwide today." (Chiou, Huang, and Lee 2005, 161) Indeed, piracy might be a greater problem internationally than it is domestically. For example, as recently as 2008, the cassette culture in Indonesia was strongly influenced by piracy and "the actual ratio of legitimate cassettes sold to pirated copies sold was about 1:8." (Wallach 2008, 16) Many commentators see this culture as being destructive to creativity.

This is not a universally held feeling, though. Some musicians are not so bothered by piracy because, "if one's work is pirated, it indicates that one's music has achieved a measure of mass acceptance." (Wallach 2008, 88) Robert Easley suggests that the music industry's response to piracy "may be holding back the evolution of the music industry towards an ultimately beneficial embrace of the possibilities inherent in electronic distribution of music." (Easley 2005, 163) The reasoning behind his contention is that these emerging technologies that enable pirating, which he refers to as "disruptive technologies," represent opportunities. Much like companies such as Kodak that based their existence on technologies that have become outdated, the music industry runs the risk of being "left behind when the market moves en masse to a new technology." Easley sees this as an opportunity, though, because "there is clear evidence of a willingness to pay for online music in general, via legal download services." (164)

Emerging technologies provide an interesting lens through which to look at piracy, though. How does YouTube relate to copyright and piracy? Lucas Hilderbrandt cynically suggested that it didn't until YouTube was purchased by Google and had enough influence and money to make it worth suing (Hilderbrandt 2007) YouTube provides a method by which users may share videos around the world instantly, providing a forum both for the ready exchange of ideas and violations of copyright. Napster, of course, is one of the other high-profile examples of a technology that made it possible to similarly share media, providing a forum for new bands to distribute their music to a larger international audience, but also providing the means for consumers to download copyrighted music without paying for the right to do so. Raymond Shih Ray Ku described this interplay between digital technologies and copyright law as a "digital dilemma." (Ku 2002, 263) While piracy and the relationship between rights holders and the consumer is one of the major aspects of copyright law, and a hotly contested one, the other major issue has to deal with the relationship between rights holders and subsequent authors.

With respect to that relationship, "copyright is vital to the existence of the music industry because the industry is based upon ownership of... songs and recordings." (Moser and Slay 2012, 10) It can be logically argued that infringement on copyright, with respect to stealing the creative ideas of others and presenting them as your own, poses as great a threat to creative production as does piracy. This is why copyright protection is seen by many as vital to the protection of creativity and as an incentive for authors[5] to continue to create.

This proposition is not without its counter-arguments, though. David Moser and Cheryl Slay note that one argument against copyright law "is that since it is often large companies rather than authors who end up owning copyrighted works, copyright law does not really provide much incentive for authors to create." (Moser and Slay 2012, 7) This is significant because "copyright exists to provide incentives for authors to produce works and thereby avoid the underproduction that might otherwise result." (Wu 2004, 281). Because of the fact that large companies generally

---

[5] A term that includes musicians in the context of copyright law.

own exclusive rights, copyright law does not really protect the musician as much as it protects the record company. Matt Stahl addresses this when comparing the successful recording artist with lesser-known musicians who sign with major labels in acknowledging that musicians "typically work under unequal contracts and must hand over long-term control of the songs and albums they produce to their record companies." (Stahl 2013, 2) He characterizes the employment relationship between musicians and record companies as "contractual bondage."

This was a common trope amongst my informants, who all communicated the experience of not seeing much economic benefit in producing recordings as most of the revenues, and profit, went to the record companies. They all seemed to feel that copyright protection was important to them as musicians, though, because of some abstract idea about how copyright protects their economic interests. When asking about the importance of copyright, Matt responded by telling me that, "I think the concept of paying someone for their art, to use their art, to borrow their art, to whatever, is a good concept. I think it needs to be that way." (Interview, December 29, 2012) Sarah, the jazz vocalist who has recorded two albums but also written a couple of songs protected by copyright, told me, "I think copyright is important because it protects artists, but it mostly protects artists who are really well known." (Interview, November 10, 2012) Sarah's comments underscore the difference between celebrity musicians and work-a-day musicians. This difference exists not just financially, but in terms of artistic freedom as well.

If I sound a bit cynical about the way my informants perceive the importance of copyright protection to their economic interests, it is because I am to a certain extent. This mild cynicism comes from the misconception that musicians actually make money off of their music. There are a number of potential revenue streams available to musicians and it is worth distinguishing them at this time to better understand which ones are, or should be, most important to musicians. First, of course, there is copyright. Copyright provides for a payment to the rights holder any time someone wants to play, perform, or use a protected work. In most cases, for example with ASCAP or BMI, a radio station pays a lump sum to one company for the right to play any songs distributed by that company and the company distributes those revenues to the rights holder. Sometimes, though, as in the case of commercial endorsements, a single lump sum is paid to the rights holder directly for the right to use a song on a limited basis known as synch rights. This operates in conjunction with the second potential revenue stream for musicians, payment for producing recordings. This represents the lump sum (sometimes in conjunction with a share of proceeds from record sales) that a musician is paid to walk into the studio and make an album. This can be thought of as part of the payment for granting exclusive rights to the record company, but it can also be considered its own revenue stream and a rather significant one.

Musicians can also earn revenue through concerts or gigging. A concert tour is separate from a record deal (although they can be lumped together) and payment for this might include a lump sum, a share of the gate (or ticket revenues), or a combination of the two. This also ties into non-musical revenue streams, such as t-shirts, other merchandising proceeds, and multimedia products and revenue streams (mobile phone apps, as an example).[6] Musicians are aware of these different potential revenue streams, too. Sarah told me she believes that music consumers, "want an experience. I mean, we live in such a world where people don't just listen to music much anymore. It's this multi-sensory thing and people love to feel like everything is virtual, everything is like right there before you in this one single package." (Interview, November 10,

---

[6] While it is not a primary focus of this thesis, Matt Stahl's book *Unfree Masters: Recording Artists and the Politics of Work* provides a thorough examination into the relationship between musicians and record companies.

2012) Royalties from use, then, are only a small potential portion of the types of revenues available to musicians. The Future of Music Coalition prepared a report detailing revenue streams for musicians and identified 42 distinct revenue streams. These fall under the main categories of Songwriter and Composer Revenue, Performer and Recording Artist Revenue, Performer Session Musician Revenue, Knowledge of Craft: Teaching and Producing, Brand-Related Revenue, Fan, Corporate and Foundation Funding, and Other Sources of Revenue. (Future 2014)

Another argument against copyright law is that one of the things the law considers infringement is what some refer to as "transformative appropriation," or "the act of referring to or quoting old works in order to create a new work." This practice "historically functioned in a spirit of sharing, friendly competition, and homage" and was quite common prior to the application of copyright law to musical works. (Demers 2006, 4) Consider the works of Mozart, Beethoven, or any other Western art music composer who has ever written a Theme and Variations. Such compositions would not be permissible under current copyright law without first paying an often exorbitant amount of money to some record company for the right to make them.

These competing arguments represent the issues present in the bulk of copyright scholarship, but the issue of copyright and identity has only briefly been touched upon. Thomas Turino stated "music is a key resource for realizing personal and collective identities which, in turn, are crucial for social, political, and economic participation." (Turino 1999, 221) Music is so closely tied to our identity, both as a society and as individuals, that it is nearly impossible to separate the two.

From a legal perspective, intellectual property law (specifically, copyright law for music) is thought to protect a product: a musician's music in this context. This formulation of materiality distinguishes "idea from concrete expression, with only the latter being subject to ownership rights as a form of property." (Easley 2005, 5) Music, of course, is one of the objects of the legal mechanism protecting intellectual property, but how does that relate to identity? The "right of publicity," a cause of action that is outside of the purview of copyright law but still closely related, serves as a marker for the development of copyright law. It has evolved through case law from protecting first a somewhat concrete object, the image of an artist, to protecting an artist's very identity and ideology. The doctrine of moral rights has developed along similar lines.

The History of Copyright Law

Copyright has a long history, both in the United States and internationally. While international copyright law differs from American copyright law in many respects, there are still certain lessons that we can take from international copyright law and apply domestically. But before delving into the international arena (or the domestic, for that matter), it is important to understand from where the concept of copyright and intellectual property derives. Conceptually speaking, a copyright, as applied to music, "is a bundle of rights (and) unless the song owner gives permission (referred to as a 'license') or unless a law permits its use, no other person can record, sell, copy, or publicly perform the song." (Stim 2009, 171) As property, a song is subject to any use or misuse that any other property is subject to, including theft. One might then say that the prohibition against infringing on copyright began in the bible with the commandment that "Thou shalt not steal."

The development of copyright law experienced a brief lull in its development between the bible and the sixteenth century, though. It was at that time that "several factors combined to turn copyright into a legal issue" at this time. Those factors included "the emerging sense of individualism... a period of rapid economic expansion carried by a new class of international merchants... (and) the invention of technology enabling fast and efficient reproduction of ideas." (Kretschmer and Kawohl 2004, 22) One might consider this a "perfect storm" of social and economic factors that not only enabled more widespread dissemination of ideas and creative products, but also the economic exploitation of those products. It was then necessary for the law to respond to these new exploitations and provide the protections that justice deemed most appropriate.

The Statute of Anne was the first legislative enactment that vested property rights with authors, as opposed to publishers.[7] It is interesting to note that the term "copyright" derives from the 1557 Licensing Act in England, "which recorded who owned the 'copy-right' (i.e. the right to print copies of the work)." Copyright, therefore, was the literal right to copy something exclusively for a set period of time. As for the Statute of Anne, it was passed on behalf of, and to benefit, the Stationers' Company "to allow them to profit from publishing, but also to provide authors with incentives to create new works." (Moser and Slay 2012, 15) The Statute of Anne extended publishing rights in existing books for 21 years while granting authors ownership rights in new works for 14 years. It is important to note that one of the original forces driving the creation of copyright law was the notion that it would promote creativity, not stifle it. It is also

---

[7] The primary publisher involved in the development of the licensing laws (the precursor to copyright law) and copyright law was the Stationers' Company.

worth noting the relatively short duration of copyright protection. The reasoning behind that short period was that expiration of the copyright would permit later authors to create derivative works through transformative appropriation without fear of sanction, thereby promoting creativity and production. It was, therefore, as important to grant exclusive copy rights as it was to limit the duration of those rights.

The implications of this reasoning, providing authors with incentives to create new works, have been at the crux of the rationale for establishing copyright law, and later for expanding its protections, since its inception. It is believed by many that copyright law encourages innovation and creation by protecting the financial interests of the author. In other words, a musician can enjoy the financial benefit of his creation for a prescribed period of time, so there is a financial incentive to create. Others would say that precluding people from expounding upon established ideas actually prevents innovation and creation by preventing access to raw material that could otherwise be transformed into new and original works. I intentionally use the term "original" here when referring to something clearly derivative because everything is derivative. Original creation has not existed since the creation of the universe and every "creation" is nothing more than the discovery of a new way to combine things that already exist. In fact, there is no way to be certain that even the creation of the universe was an original act. The Big Bang had to be an explosion of *something* and the idea for the heavens and earth by a supreme being surely also came from somewhere.

The first American copyright statute was the Copyright Act of 1790, which was based largely on the Statute of Anne. The most significant development in American copyright law after enactment of the 1790 act occurred when "President Theodore Roosevelt called for a complete revision of the Copyright Act in order to bring it in line with technological advances that had taken place." After all, it was technological development that necessitated the creation of copyright law in the first place, so it was only sensible that copyright law evolve to incorporate developments in the technologies of production. This resulted in the Copyright Act of 1909, which extended protection beyond writings and into the realm of "works that are based upon the creative powers of the mind and are the fruits of intellectual labor." (Moser and Slay 2012, 18) Copyright protection under this act lasted for 28 years with an available renewal of equal length. This was the first statute that covered musical, as well as literary, publications.

The latest significant overhaul to copyright law in the United States occurred with passage of the Copyright Act of 1976. This eliminated the registration requirement, meaning that works were copyrighted when they were fixed in a tangible form, broadened the coverage of copyright, changed the duration of copyright to 70 years after the death of the author for new works and 28 years after the enactment of the law for existing works still under copyright protection with an available renewal for an additional 67 years, and codified the fair use doctrine, among other things. Fair use is a somewhat less than clear concept as the statute does not explicitly define it. Even "the legislative history to the Copyright Act stated that the fair use doctrine is 'an equitable rule of reason' and, as such, is not susceptible to any 'generally applicable definition.'" (Moser and Slay 2012, 208)

Since the 1976 Act, there have been several amendments to the act and new laws passed to account for developments in use and technology.[8] In 1989, the United States also finally became a member of "that preeminent international copyright treaty, the Berne Convention for the Protection of Literary and Artistic Works." (Nimmer et al. 2005, 2) The Berne Convention

---

[8] For example, the Audio Home Recording Act of 1992, the Performance Right in Sound Recordings Act of 1995, the No Electronic Theft Act of 1997, and the Digital Millennium Copyright Act of 1998, among others.

does establish some rights, such as moral rights, but it exists primarily as a union of participating countries providing copyright protection and an enforcement framework to foreign works created in member countries. The Berne Convention Implementation Act of 1988, however, provides that the act does not expand or reduce any rights granted to authors by operation of law in America. The Berne Convention, therefore, does not change domestic copyright protection; it only provides reciprocal rights between member nations.

The United States was a latecomer to the idea of international rights, though, as the Berne Convention was originally passed in 1886. One might wonder why the United States was so reluctant to respond to international developments in copyright law, but there is no simple answer. American jurisprudence is based upon European law, but has developed independently and European case law has little value in American courts. This self-imposed legal isolation is not unique to copyright law; copyright is just a victim of it. Christopher Sprigman suggests that another rationale for America's late accession to the Berne Convention was "the Convention's prohibition of formalities." (Sprigman 2004, 540) An example of these "formalities" would include the registration requirement, but it should be noted that there was already no registration requirement in the 1976 Act, passed 12 years before America subscribed to the Berne Convention. By the time Congress passed the Berne Convention Implementation Act of 1988, American copyright law was already responding to external influence, including developments in international copyright law, and the writing was on the wall for a gradual change in American copyright law toward conformity with international copyright law, which brings us to today.

Today, statutory copyright law in the form of the Copyright Act of 1976 is covered in Title 17 of the United States Code. The cornerstone of Title 17 is the section defining the scope of the statute, 17 USC 102. It states that "copyright protection subsists, in accordance with this title, in original works of authorship fixed in any tangible medium of expression." This establishes two criteria for copyright protection to apply: that the work be original and that it be fixed. There is no registration requirement for copyright to attach. Chapter 1 of Title 17 also establishes a few limitations on exclusive rights, in other words it provides for some uses to which copyright does not apply or applies in a limited manner. Some of these include reproduction by libraries and archives (§108), transfers of recordings (§109), or certain performances or displays (§110), but the most significant exemptions from exclusive rights copyright protection is fair use (§107)

The Fair Use Doctrine was originally a judicial creation but was incorporated into the statute in 1976 and amended twice since then (in 1990 and in 1992). The Fair Use Doctrine holds that any use of copyrighted material "for purposes such as criticism, comment, news reporting, teaching (including multiple copies for classroom use), scholarship, or research, is not an infringement of copyright." In determining whether a particular use is a fair use, the statute sets forth four criteria to consider: the purpose and character of the use, the nature of the work, the amount used, and the effect on the potential market for the work. It is this third criterion that allows for the use of "samples" of limited duration in new musical works. It is left to the court to interpret fair use and its scope through judicial decisions.[9]

Most of the criticism of copyright revolves around copyright ownership. Title 17 establishes that copyright protection vests in the author or authors of the copyrighted work. In the case of works for hire, though, the person for whom the work was created is considered the owner. Exclusive rights may also be transferred, though, and that is the crux of the criticism. Under the traditional model of the recording industry, the large record companies possess a

---

[9] For more on fair use and sampling, see Kembrew McLeod and Peter DiCola's *Creative License: The Law and Culture of Digital Sampling.*

tremendous amount of power over musicians. The only way musicians can hope to enjoy financial success is to sign with a major label, a condition of which is to transfer exclusive rights to the record company. The record company then has the resources to market albums, ensure national radio airplay, and distribute albums to record stores. This disparity imparts great bargaining power upon the record company, making musicians "subject to the superior market power of the monopolistic league of buyers of their services and products." (Stahl 2013, 231) Musicians then have limited or no rights in their own music, sometimes even forcing them to pay for the right to remake their own songs.

The traditional model seems to be eroding as a result of technological developments and the ability of musicians to avail themselves of new grassroots distribution methods. The most successful band to eschew the traditional model is Radiohead, a European band that has been outspoken in its criticism of copyright law. They released their seventh album, *Rainbows*, as a digital download and allowed users to set their own price. Since then, Radiohead has been releasing their albums independently and has enjoyed great success. There are, of course, also many musicians who have parlayed viral success on websites such as YouTube into major record deals and significant financial success, the most obvious of which is Justin Bieber.

Modern technology, however, has given rise to the DIY (Do It Yourself) movement, where musicians and bands are using home recording and editing equipment to create albums and utilizing alternative distribution methods, such as iTunes and YouTube, to distribute their albums and generate buzz about their music. This movement is also known as the Direct-to-Fan business model. Examples include major names such as Radiohead and Trent Reznor (who is now back with a major record label) and smaller niche genres such a filk.

Some of the resources available for DIY bands include social networking sites like Facebook and MySpace, band websites, blogs, fan involvement, email campaigns, digital distribution on iTunes or Amazon, and companies that assist with the DIY process, providing marketing services to these bands for a fee while letting the bands retain rights in the content. This movement does not exist exclusively in music, though. Print publishing is being challenged by digital versions of books and self-publishing services that will print books on demand and provide services to authors, such as distribution through Amazon and traditional brick-and-mortar stores, as well as marketing solutions. All of these alternative business models provide higher margins for authors and musicians, making such models desirable. Still, as Trent Rezner's example illustrates, major record labels provide the most expedient method for widespread distribution and recognition and remain the preferred model of distribution and marketing for most musicians. And, since musicians do not make the bulk of their money from copyright royalties, but rather from record sales, concert revenues, and other revenue streams, major record labels still wield tremendous power over musicians.

Another criticism of copyright law relates to the duration of copyright. Currently, exclusive rights in a copyrighted work last for the life of the author (or last surviving author) plus 70 years for works created after January 1, 1978 (the effective date of the 1976 Act). For earlier works with existing copyrights, the term of the copyright was fixed at 28 years and was eligible for a renewal for a further 67 years. This is a far cry from the Statute of Anne, which set exclusive rights in new works at a flat 14 years and existing works for 21 years. This expansion was the result of pressure by major copyright holders to expand those rights so they did not lose them. This not only limits the ability of authors to create derivative works, but also protects the substantial interests of major record companies, while not providing much benefit for original authors. Some see this as a way to perpetuate a flawed system and discourage production of new original works.

An alternative theory of the purposes of copyright law was suggested by Attorney Timothy Wu, who suggested that there were two focuses of copyright law: authorship and communication. The authorship regime is the one that we are most familiar with where the law is primarily focused on protecting the author (or exclusive rights owner) of the work. Under the communication regime, the focus is on the dissemination of ideas. Timothy Wu suggests that, since 1976, "new sections of the law regulating competition among disseminators have emerged as a response to a transformation in the nature of the challenge of incumbents." (Wu 2004, 280) He explains that the communication theory of copyright law exists because of the existing conflict between authors, disseminators, and consumers. They are "in relationships made up of repeat interactions fraught with potential for conflict and abusive behavior." This communication theory exists as a kind of "antitrust policy as between disseminators." (286)

Regardless of the effect of copyright law on creation, it exists as a powerful force in American law. In my fieldwork, I found a general sentiment that musicians felt that copyright protection was important, but could not express specific ways in which it actually protected them. Tom believes that, "if not for copyright protection, many artists would not be able to work and make a living for their families." (Interview, December 19, 2012) Will believed that, "all artists should be treated fairly in the legal system. Especially as it pertains to ownership of music," providing a justification for the importance of copyright law. (Interview, January 5, 2013) As I have illustrated throughout this basic introduction to copyright law, though, the interests that are actually protected by the law are not necessarily those of the musician. I am not suggesting that copyright law should be changed, I am merely pointing out some of the practical implications of copyright law in the creative environment.

Copyright and Identity: Making the Connection

I have previously argued that voice is an integral part of identity. This discussion of copyright law ultimately ties back into identity because the ideological voice represents the outward manifestation of our identity to the world. This cultural force is particularly significant where we are considering someone with enough cultural cache to affect social change, both positive and negative. That person then acts as a focal point for the creation of cultural or identity cohorts. Cultural cohorts are especially influential when they grow out of a perceived affinity with the perceived identity of a celebrity. Idolization of musicians often leads to changes in the behavior and beliefs of cohort members to conform to those behaviors perceived to be in consonance with the musician's.

This is demonstrated most effectively when we consider celebrity scandals and how fans often feel betrayed by them. There is probably no better example of this principle in action than the Milli Vanilli scandal and the feelings of betrayal that the group's fans felt upon learning that the faces of the marketing of the group were not actually the people doing the singing. Of course, the music was the same music fans had grown to love, but they were outraged at the perceived betrayal perpetrated by the band and the record company. This was a clear demonstration of how identity is sometimes more important with respect to a musician than his music.

This danger is very real when it relates to the musician's own actions, but is equally significant when the musician's identity is assailed by others. These assaults often serve as a galvanizing force within the cohort creating something of a bunker mentality. Having said that, identity can be thought of as a tool that the musician can wield to affect positive or negative change. As I have argued earlier, it also serves as a tool that can provide the type of economic benefit to the musician that his music simply cannot. Protection of this economic interest is why it is important to musicians for the law to protect not only their work product, or their music, but also to protect their identity.

It is remarkable the type of antagonism, or at least mistrust, that exists between musicians and record labels. All of my informants shared the opinion that copyright was really nothing more than a tool used to protect the record companies and held little real benefit for them. This tension was best reflected in my informant who was involved in the production side of music, as well as the creation side. When I approached him to explain my project and ask for his participation, his fear was almost palpable as he eyed me with distrust and insisted upon his absolute anonymity. It was clear to me that he was greatly concerned with how his career might suffer if any major record companies discovered he had said anything they might perceive as disparaging against them or the record industry. Despite my insistence that his identity would be protected, I sensed that he was censoring himself throughout our interview for fear of saying something that might come back to haunt him later. This fear and self-censorship has implications with respect to the veracity and usefulness of fieldwork in general, but most immediately served to illustrate the power record companies wield and the fear that power engenders.

Copyright law has not developed in a manner that enables protection of the musician's interest in his identity, though, and typical civil law does not help, either. Libel and slander really only apply where someone has explicitly made false statements, either verbally or in writing, about someone. That certainly has implications relative to identity, but it does not protect against

the most insidious attacks on identity. There are two legal concepts in domestic and international

copyright law, though, that do and they are slowly being incorporated into American

jurisprudence: the right of publicity and the moral rights doctrine.

CHAPTER III
THE RIGHT OF PUBLICITY: FROM ITS ORIGINS TO TODAY[10]

Joseph Stamets wrote a law review article on the "right of publicity" in 1990 where he

discussed the historical development of the right and, what he considers, the troubling way it was

applied to a high-profile case involving Tom Waits. He rightly points out that the right of

publicity arose out of the already well-established right of privacy tort and it has become fairly

widely accepted as a hybrid of the common-law causes of action of right of privacy and

misappropriation, but I disagree with his conclusions and outline what I consider the

development of the right of publicity since its inception and its implication for identity studies

today in this chapter.

The right of publicity was necessary because the right of privacy did not really apply to

celebrities. One of the main casebooks[11] on copyright law explains that this is because they "do

not seek the 'solitude and privacy' which (courts) sought to protect. Indeed, privacy is the one

thing they do 'not want, or need.' Their concern is rather with publicity, which may be regarded

as the reverse side of the coin of privacy." (Nimmer et al. 2006, 1195) While there is no single

statement of what the right of publicity covers, the Restatement (Third) of Unfair Competition

provides instruction. Restatements are books published by the American Law Institute intended

to provide instruction to legal professionals, but they are not binding precedent. §46 of the

Restatement states that "one who appropriates the commercial value of a person's identity by

---

[10] The bulk of this chapter is extracted from an upcoming article to be published in *Popular Music and Society* (Klein forthcoming) and is used here by permission of the publisher.
[11] A casebook is the name for a textbook used in law school.

using without consent the person's name, likeness, or other indicia of identity for purposes of trade is subject to liability." (Restatement 1993, 8)

Throughout its existence, the right of publicity has developed in three phases. The first was as a shortcut around contract and intellectual property law. The second was as a type of unjust enrichment substitute. The final phase, which is where the cause of action stands today, incorporates both of those approaches while also recognizing that there is something more that the right of publicity is capable of protecting, and that is a musician's identity. I begin this chapter by providing a brief summary of the first two phases of the right of publicity's development before moving on to explore the final developmental phase: the one that has ethnomusicological implications and should be of prime importance to musicians.

The First Phase of the Right of Publicity

The first phase of right of publicity cases was relatively limited in scope and protected only tangible representations, such as visual likenesses or catch-phrases. One of the first cases to recognize the right of publicity was *Haelan Laboratories v. Topps Chewing Gum, Inc.*, a 1953 case where a professional baseball player entered into an exclusive contract with a chewing gum company for that company to use his likeness to advertise its product. Topps Chewing Gum, Inc. later entered into a contract with that same baseball player to use his photograph to sell its chewing gum. Haelan Laboratories sued Topps as a third-party defendant for violation of its publicity interest in using the baseball player's likeness.

Haelan Laboratories is fairly limited in its general applicability, aside from the fact that it marks the official beginning of the jurisprudence of the right of publicity as separate from the right of privacy. The Court held that the right of publicity exists "in addition to and independent of that right of privacy." The Court's rationale for recognizing the right of publicity was that "many prominent persons… would feel sorely deprived if they no longer received money for authorizing advertisements, popularizing their countenances." (Haelan 1953, 868) While this application is relatively limited in its scope, it has been expanded since that time.

Shortly after *Haelan Laboratories* in 1960, Dean Prosser published a law review article explaining the right of publicity in relation to the right of privacy. He wrote that the right of privacy has four separate types, which include "(1) intrusion upon one's seclusion or solitude, (2) public disclosure of embarrassing private facts, (3) publicity which places one in a false light, and (4) appropriation of one's name or likeness for the defendant's advantage." (Prosser 1960, 389) The right of publicity, then, was recognized as a subset of the right of privacy and encompassed the third and fourth of Prosser's types of privacy. Prosser has become one of the most oft-cited secondary sources in right of publicity cases and forms the basis of right of publicity jurisprudence.

A later case representative of the trend of first phase right of publicity cases is the 1983 case of *John W. Carson v. Here's Johnny Portable Toilets, Inc.*, a case where famous talk show host Johnny Carson sued a Michigan portable toilet company for using the phrase "Here's Johnny," a phrase that had long been associated with Mr. Carson, in its company name and advertisements. The right of publicity claim was brought in conjunction with a Lanham Act claim[12] where plaintiff characterized the phrase as a trademark and, therefore, protected. The right of publicity in this first phase is almost always pled in conjunction with the Lanham Act and, where the right of publicity is found to be the appropriate cause of action, the Lanham Act

---

[12] The Lanham Act (15 USC §1501, *et seq.*) deals with trademark protection.

claims are usually dismissed. This is typical of pleading in civil actions. Attorneys must generally plead all possible causes of action when they file or they may lose the right to bring them later. A civil complaint, then, becomes something of a game of throwing spaghetti at the wall and seeing what sticks. Plaintiffs often plead dozens of different counts and causes of action with the knowledge that only one or two of them may survive a motion for summary judgment (a type of motion to dismiss).

The Court, as is typical in these types of cases, upheld the dismissal of the Lanham Act claim, but found a violation of the common law right of publicity. The Court held that "the right of publicity, as we have stated, is that a celebrity has a protected pecuniary interest in the commercial exploitation of his identity. If the celebrity's identity is commercially exploited, there has been an invasion of his right whether or not his 'name or likeness' is used." (Carson 1983, 835) As an interesting side note, the Court also acknowledged Carson's claim that he was "embarrassed by and considers it odious to be associated with the appellee's product." (834) This section of the court's opinion is what is known as *dicta*, or extra content that does not constitute binding precedent, but can nonetheless be instructive to later courts. As *dicta*, that was not recognized as a part of Carson's right to privacy, but it is the beginning of a line of reasoning that finds its culmination in the third phase of right of publicity cases.

The Second Phase of the Right of Publicity

By the 1980s, the right of publicity had entered its second phase of cases where the cause was generally looked upon as a type of unjust enrichment. Unjust enrichment is an action between two parties who do not have a contract, but where one has benefitted from the actions, and has not fairly compensated, the other. An example of unjust enrichment might be where a house painter mistakenly paints the wrong house while the homeowner watches and does not stop the painter. There is no contract between the two because the painter's contract was actually with the neighbor, but one has enjoyed a benefit of the other's services without paying for them. A recovery is still allowed, but since there is no actual contract between the parties, unjust enrichment is considered a quasi-contractual action. This is just a summary of unjust enrichment and there are more elements to the cause of action, but for now, a summary will suffice.

When New York first recognized a non-statutory cause of action for right of publicity in 1981,[13] it defined the action as "the right of an individual to control the commercial value of his name and likeness and to prevent their unauthorized exploitation by others." (Marx 1981, 487) This is an interesting definition because it limits recovery to situations where only the name or likeness of a celebrity has been misappropriated. The *Marx* case was primarily about whether a right of publicity claim was descendible, meaning whether it would pass on to the victim's descendants after death, but it also addressed the reasoning behind the claim in the first place. The Court recognized that the Marx Brothers

> earned their livelihoods by exploiting the unique characters they created... (and) there
> can be no question of intent to capitalize on the commercial value of artificial
> personalities created for entertainment purposes. Every appearance, contract and
> advertisement involving the Marx Brothers signified a recognition by the performers of
> the commercial value of the unique characters they portrayed. (491)

This marks one of the first times a court of law recognized that there is some tangible value to a persona. The *Marx* court, then, placed a value on that persona and recognized that

---

[13] A case where the Estate of the Marx Brothers sued a company that produced a play where the performers simulated the unique styles of the Marx Brothers.

someone making unauthorized use of that persona was unjustly enriched by its actions. This was, therefore, a situation where one party enjoyed an economic benefit by exploiting something the plaintiffs had intentionally developed as a tool for commercial gain. Stamets dances around the significance of this nuance where he discusses the *Marx* case in relation to Elvis impersonators and distinguishes the two cases as treating "performance style as a kind of animate likeness... (while) a right of publicity in abstractable personality qualities – such as sneezing comically or dancing like Fred Astaire – has yet to surface to support advocates for a right of publicity in performance style." (Stamets 2012, 352)

This analysis misses the point that the *Marx* case protected something artificially created specifically for commercial gain, while situations like those involving Elvis impersonators involve impersonations of an individual's general demeanor and not something intentionally crafted for a pecuniary purpose. In a sense, the court looked at the Marx personas as artificial commercial creations while viewing Elvis's persona as something natural (although that distinction is arguable). Under current law, impersonators are protected under the First Amendment because the impersonation is performed as a sort of parody designed to entertain and the intent is not to deceive or mislead the audience into believing it is not an impersonation. Put another way, "the difference between a 'parody' and a 'knock-off' is the difference between fun and profit." (White 1992, 1401) In other words, impersonators are intentionally and obviously performing as impersonators.

While first phase cases were generally brought in tandem with Lanham Act claims, second phase cases were frequently pled in conjunction with misappropriation. This is not, in and of itself, significant with respect to what constitutes a cause of action for violation of the right of publicity, but it does suggest the growth that was occurring in the case law with respect to that cause of action. Initially, the right of publicity was viewed as a tangible thing, akin to a trademark or other intellectual property. By the second phase, the courts had begun to think of a celebrity's persona as a tangible thing in and of itself and something with value that could be stolen or misappropriated.

The Third Phase of the Right of Publicity

The third phase of the right of publicity began with *Midler v. Ford Motor Company* in 1988 and represents an expansion of the right of publicity that finally begins to shed some light on what exactly the right of publicity should be protecting. It is in this phase that ethnomusicological understandings of voice and identity come into play. While some cases are still decided with reasoning that is consistent with the first two phases,[14] courts seem to be more concerned with exploitation of intangibles such as personality, identity, voice, or ideology than simply photographs or likenesses.

In *Midler*, Ford Motor Company through its ad agency, Young & Rubicam, approached Bette Midler with the intent to retain her to sing for its commercials. After the briefest of discussions, Ms. Midler refused to agree to sing for those commercials, so Young & Rubicam retained a Bette Midler sound-alike to sing the well-known 1972 Midler song "Do You Want to Dance" for the commercials. Upon learning of the commercials, Midler sued both Ford and Young & Rubicam claiming a violation of her right of publicity.[15] This is a unique case because

---

[14] See, for example, *Jim Henson Productions, Inc. v. John T. Brady & Associates, Inc.*, 867 F.Supp 175 (SD NY 1994) where the court applied an unjust enrichment reasoning.
[15] It should be noted that, where an advertising agency is responsible for producing the advertisement, both the agency and the company it is representing are liable under theories of

it is the first case that only addresses the right of publicity, rather than being linked with another cause of action.

The Court ruled in Ms. Midler's favor, holding that "a voice is more distinctive and more personal than the automobile accoutrements protected (previously). A voice is as distinctive and personal as a face. The human voice is one of the most palpable ways identity is manifested."[16] (Midler 1988, 463) This is significant because it marks the first time a court made such a strong connection between voice and identity and the first time they were considered as justification for legal action. Philip Auslander characterizes this case as "an explicit effort to protect performance in ways not possible under federal copyright." (Auslander 1999, 161) While he is correct that federal copyright protection does not protect the interests at issue in the *Midler* case, it is not really Ms. Midler's performance in the traditional sense that the court was protecting. In the sense that identity is, in itself, a type of performance manifested through voice, though, Auslander's position is correct.

Voice and identity is a connection that ethnomusicologists are well aware of. Simon Frith, for example, has noted that "the voice, in short, may or may not be the key to someone's identity, but it is certainly the key to the ways in which we change identities." (Frith 1996, 197) The *Midler* court was very progressive, even quoting Don Ihde's seminal work on voice, *Listening and Voice*, in its opinion. The use of that book marked the first time an opinion in a right of publicity case looked further afield than simply other case law, restatements of law, or

---

agency law. Of the cases discussed in this article, this is the first where an advertising agency has been implicated.

[16] The "automobile accoutrements" noted by the court refers to an earlier case where the likeness of a famous race car driver's car was used in an advertisement and features of the car, specifically its white pinpointing, an oval medallion, and its color, were not changed, potentially leading people to believe the driver had endorsed the product.

legal publications to arrive at a deeper understanding of why the cause of action exists and what it ought to protect.

Midler is also interesting because it is factually similar to an earlier case involving Nancy Sinatra, (Sinatra 1970) which had a different result than *Midler*. In *Sinatra*, Goodyear used Sinatra's famous song "These Boots are Made for Walking" in advertisements for its "wide boots" tire design. The advertising company secured the rights to use the song, but chose a Nancy Sinatra sound-alike after unsuccessfully attempting to sign Sinatra herself. Factually, this sounds almost identical to *Midler*, also a Ninth Circuit case, yet the *Sinatra* court found no liability on Sinatra's right of publicity claim.

The main difference and, it turns out, the dispositive difference between the two cases, was that a third party owned the rights to the song in *Sinatra* and had duly licensed those rights to Goodyear and that Sinatra was only objecting to the use of a similar arrangement of the song and not the fact that the singer sounded like her. Sinatra claimed "that said song and the arrangement used by defendants 'has acquired a secondary meaning' [that was appropriated and designed to] deceive the public." (Sinatra 1970, 712) That was not enough to impose liability on Goodyear because of the fact that Goodyear had rightfully obtained the rights to the song and a finding of liability would have violated copyright protection. The copyright holder had absolute control over the song and, in fact, the court pointed out that Sinatra herself "was required to obtain permission from the copyright owner to sing 'Boots,' and to make an arrangement of the song to suit her own tastes and talents." (716)

The *Midler* court noted that, "if Midler were claiming a secondary meaning to 'Do You Want To Dance' or seeking to prevent defendants from using that song, she would fail like

Sinatra." (Midler 1988, 462) On paper, that is why Midler succeeded where Sinatra failed.[17]

That conclusion is troubling, though, because Young & Rubicam also owned the rights to

perform the song, so there is really little difference, if any, between *Sinatra* and *Midler*. So what

accounts for the apparently conflicting decisions? In reality, this is likely a situation where the

Court recognized that case law was not developing in a manner consistent with protecting

everything the right of publicity should be protecting. Richard McEwen, in comparing both the

Midler and the *Sinatra* cases, concluded that "the *Midler* result is more satisfying than *Sinatra*

because it acknowledges the value of performance and provides a mechanism for performers to

maintain legal control over its appropriation." (McEwen 1994, 128) This is consistent with the

underlying aims of the legal process in general.

One of the most influential statements on the underlying aims of the legal process came

from Harvard Law School professors Henry Hart and Albert Sacks. They claimed that, "in the

satisfaction of all their wants, people are continuously and inescapably dependent upon one

another." (Hart and Sacks 1994, 1) Therefore, the three main objectives of any institutional

system are "to avoid the disintegration of social order,… to maximize the total satisfactions of

valid human wants, [and] the *pragmatic necessity* of a currently fair division." (104) These

objectives are actually closely related in that ensuring a currently fair division maximizes the

total satisfactions of valid human wants, which prevents the disintegration of social order.[18]

---

[17] Like in *Sinatra*, Young & Rubicam had acquired the right to use the song, just not the artist's voice.
[18] Having been both an attorney and an ethnomusicologist, I have observed a significant difference between the ways the two camps view the legal system. Ethnomusicologists often view the legal system as a tool of capitalist power and domination while attorneys see it as a tool to promote justice and equity. While this is, indeed, a fertile field for discussion, it falls somewhat outside the scope of this study and will not be addressed here.

All of these objectives are tied up in the generally understood notions of justice and equity that most people associate with the legal system and *Midler* satisfies each of them. If the system failed to protect Midler's voice, it would threaten the three objectives by making it more appealing for others in a similar situation as Ford Motor Company to exploit the voices and identities of other celebrities in the future. This also demonstrates why the First Amendment does not afford the defendants protection in these instances. The First Amendment does not provide immunity where the use is merely exploitative. (Midler 1988) I believe it can also be implied that the First Amendment does not apply where the purpose is to mislead, confuse, or defraud the public, as in the *Midler* case. These considerations justify the "expansion" of the case law Stamets observed beginning with the *Midler* case.

This expansion brings us to the most significant case in all of right of publicity jurisprudence: the 1992 *Waits* case. Tom Waits had a long-standing and public disdain for advertising, feeling that artists detract from their artistic integrity by doing commercials. In fact, his distaste for the practice was so strong he wrote a song criticizing the practice called "Step Right Up." Frito-Lay's advertising agency, Tracy-Locke, Inc., apparently missing the memo that the song was an indictment upon the advertising industry, wanted to hire Waits to sing a song that ironically mimicked "Step Right Up" for one of its commercials. Waits, naturally, refused and Tracy-Locke then hired a sound-alike to sing the song. What makes matters worse is that the advertising agency was "concerned about the legal implications of (the singer's) skill in imitating Waits [and felt] that Waits would be unhappy with the commercial because of his publicly avowed policy against doing commercial endorsements and his disapproval of artists who did." (Waits 1992, 1098) In other words, the advertising agency knew what they were doing was wrong, suspected it might expose them to liability, but did it anyway.

The court noted that "Waits' voice misappropriation claim is one for invasion of a personal property right: his right of publicity to control the use of his identity as embodied in his voice." (Waits 1992, 1100) Where the *Waits* case differs from its predecessors is that Waits sought not only economic damages, but also damages for mental distress. The court ruled that such damages were appropriate based upon the "evidence of Waits' shock, anger, and embarrassment... because of his outspoken public stance against doing commercial endorsements [which] humiliated Waits by making him an apparent hypocrite." (1103) This opposition is the crux of the rationale behind the *Waits* case and the genesis of what I call an artist's negative voice.[19]

As for the musicians I interviewed, they all acknowledged some sense of moral responsibility when dealing with endorsement. As I mentioned in my introduction, several of my informants have had their music used in some commercial setting. This has been from local and national advertising campaigns such as Chevrolet, the Detroit Zoo, Sparrow Hospitals in Lansing, Michigan, a Detroit television station, and various political campaigns, to use in television shows in both ABC's Men in Trees and as the theme of the Showtime series Shameless, and one even had one of his songs used in an eCard. None of these musicians have the distinctive voice and fame of Tom Waits, but one of them related to me that a fan had his lyrics tattooed on her body, which also speaks to the type of relationship that can exist between a cultural cohort and its leader as it is reflected in how the musician/fan dynamic is manifested.

As I mentioned, each of my informants noted some degree of moral or ethical responsibility when deciding whether to permit their music to be used in advertisements. Whether this related to their integrity amongst their fans or was just a personal decision, it is a

---

[19] Since the time of this case, Waits has successfully sued other advertisers on similar grounds, including Audi and General Motors' Opel division.

reflection on their identity and is at least implicitly related to their integrity and reputation. The most opportunistic of my informants told me that, "as long as you don't have any strong objections to the product or the way your music is used, I consider it a totally acceptable way to generate income and buzz as a musician." After being pressed further, though, he acknowledged that, "there are probably some companies or products I would turn down even for good pay. Everyone should show some integrity now and then." Other informants noted the importance of supporting the product they were being associated with. One told me that he, "would need to be familiar with a product, or have some affinity for it, before I could endorse it." Another told me that he, "would think that one has to truly support what they are endorsing." The interesting thing to me about these responses is that my question was not about endorsing a product, but rather about having their music used in commercials. They made the connection between use and endorsement, suggesting that they think of themselves as endorsing products when their music is used in advertising it.

So what would my informants do if placed in Waits' or Midler's shoes and an impersonator was used in an advertisement in a way that led the public to believe it was them singing? I laid out the Midler scenario as a hypothetical to each of them and asked them what they would do in such a situation. One gave me a rather political answer and told me that he would be, "flattered that someone would want to imitate me, but I feel that there should be some sort of acknowledgement, financial or otherwise." Another was more direct when he said that if he, "had written the song and relied on its success for (his) livelihood, and the person was intentionally trying to impersonate (him) for financial gain, then (he) would likely investigate what legal recourse (he) could take." It turns out that he likely would have some legal recourse available to him.

Since the time of Stamets' article, Minnesota has upheld the right of publicity stating that it existed to protect an individual's identity. (Feagre & Benson 2005) A Missouri court held that the right of publicity protects "a person from losing the benefit of their work in creating a publicly recognizable persona." (Bear Foot 1998) New Jersey, in an action by the Estate of Louis Prima against the Olive Garden restaurants for hiring a sound-alike to record the song "Oh Marie" for use in its commercials, affirmed the Estate's argument in favor of an "enforceable right in Prima's identity and persona." (Prima 2000, 350) These cases, even though not dealing with negative voice, are still speaking in terms of things like identity or persona, which is the primary difference between third phase right of publicity and its earlier manifestations. Richard McEwen believes that *Waits* represents a "logical step in the evolution of intellectual property law," although his analysis focuses mainly on the aspects of the case relating to the Lanham Act. (McEwen 1994, 139) Where Stamets sees this as an unjustified expansion of the right of publicity, I see it as a continuation of the natural evolution of the right of publicity. An evolution that provides greater protection to musicians and their identities and potentially tracks with the development of copyright law to include the moral rights doctrine.

CHAPTER IV
MORAL RIGHTS AND THE ETHICS OF COPYRIGHT

The judicial doctrine of the right of publicity is one that I argue has expanded to encompass the protection of a musician's ideological voice even where he does not possess exclusive rights in a copyrighted work, but this issue is far from settled. Even where it has been adopted, the boundaries of that right are not exactly clear and unambiguous. In order for that to happen, the right of publicity would have to make its way into statutory law in much the way the Fair Use Doctrine was codified. Even then, there would likely still be much room for interpretation, but at least it would be a legislative creature instead of a judicial one and would provide universal protection for a musician's ideological interests in addition to his economic interests.

American copyright law is actually somewhat unique in that it does not already provide for such statutory protection. The moral rights doctrine is such a statute and it exists in the Berne Convention and in the law of many of its member countries. Timothy Wu explains that, under what is known as the natural rights theory of copyright law, "authors have a moral right to the fruits of their labors," (Wu 2004, 282) In this chapter, I explore moral rights, the ways in which they protect musicians, and what role they play in American copyright law.

Moral Rights and Identity

The doctrine of *moral rights* is one that is relatively unfamiliar to the realm of American copyright law. As it relates to music, the doctrine of moral rights assumes that "the author of a song is considered to have some 'moral' claim to what happens to the song." (Stim 2003, 173) There are two aspects of moral rights: the right to attribution and the classic *droit moral*. It is the latter set of rights that I am going to focus on here. The moral rights doctrine has made some headway in the United States, though, beginning with the protection of visual art in California and New York.[20] California and New York are typically at the forefront of developments in the law, with the rest of the country following close behind, so we can look to these developments as harbingers of things to come elsewhere.

Basically, the moral rights doctrine presupposes that "an author is believed to be morally entitled to control and exploit the products of the author's intellect." (Moser and Slay 2012, 5) Later in this thesis, I argue in favor of the idea of an artist's negative voice, or the ability to speak by the absence of speech. The negative voice is the right that any individual, especially a celebrity, has to refuse to align himself with something as a means of protest or disassociation. This is basically what the doctrine of moral rights protects for visual artists. This principle, though, is every bit as applicable to the use of music as it is to visual art. In point of fact, music has an arguably broader scope of influence amongst cultural cohorts and society in general.

It is also worth pointing out how state law interacts with federal law where they both cover the same thing. The doctrine of preemption holds that federal law preempts state law where there is a conflict between the two. This is a simplistic description of the interplay

---

[20] See California Civil Code, Section 987 (amended in 1982) and Title C, Articles 11-14, New York Arts & Cult. Aff. Law

between federal and state law, though. A conflict only exists where state law does not provide as much protection as federal law. In such cases, state law would not serve as a defense against an action based upon federal law. States are permitted, in most instances, to provide greater protections than federal law in many areas, but where they provide lesser protections, federal law still controls. By way of a purely hypothetical example, if the federal government were to establish a national emission standard for motor vehicles, a state would be permitted to mandate a stricter standard. That state would just not be permitted to implement a lower standard. Preemption becomes particularly tricky where there are other areas of federal law, state law, or the Constitution that come into play, but it generally provides that federal trumps state law where there is a real conflict between the two.

The reason this is important is because moral rights is a case where state law in New York and California began providing greater protections than those provided by federal law to visual artists, so those laws were not preempted by federal law. The New York and California laws made their mark on the federal landscape and have led to limited adoption of moral rights on a federal level.

Demands for similar protections on a national basis after the passage of the California and New York laws led to the passage of the Visual Artists Rights Act of 1990.[21] This law does not apply to music or other copyright protected media, but only to visual arts such as panting, but the creators of these protected works are protected not only from unauthorized use of the work itself, but actions that tarnish or assail the ideology of the work. The thing that is most interesting about this doctrine is that it is actually a codified part of Title 17 copyright law, as opposed to a judicial creation. Moral rights for visual artists exist in 17 USC §106A, titled "Rights of certain

---

[21] Visual Artists Rights Act, 104 Stat. 5128 (1990)

authors to attribution and integrity." That section holds that "the author of a work of visual art…

shall have the right to prevent the use of his or her name as the author of the work of visual art in

the event of a distortion, mutilation, or other modification of the work which would be

prejudicial to his or her honor or reputation." This right lasts for the lifetime of the author (or last

surviving author) of the work, vests exclusively in the authors regardless of whether that author

retains copyright ownership or not, and may not be transferred to anyone else. This is a method

by which authors may exert some control over the use of their creations even where they have

assigned exclusive rights to that work to someone else. Christopher Sprigman notes that some of

the other methods available to original authors in America to protect their moral interests in

derivative materials include "state unfair competition, defamation, and privacy laws; and the

Visual Artists Rights Act of 1990." (Sprigman 2004, 563)

Why is there a limitation on transferability, unlike exclusive rights, and why does it

expire upon the artist's death? After all, shouldn't the author's integrity matter even after his

death? While the legislative history of the statute is not instructive in this respect, it is not

difficult to make an educated guess as to the rationale. The right is non-transferable, naturally,

because the artist is really the only person with an interest in his reputation. It is illogical to

permit transfers of this right as it could then conceivably be used to protect moral rights that

conflict with those of the author. As for the lifetime limitation, that is also not difficult to justify.

The author is the only person who can provide evidence of his own morals and what runs afoul

of them. Exclusive rights granted by copyright attach to a physical object (notes on paper or a

recording), so it is easier to define what is protected and whether it has been used or not. Morals

are not so easily bounded, so it is much more difficult to define whether a use conflicts with the

author's morals. This becomes purely speculative when the author is unavailable to provide testimony regarding those morals. That is not to say there are not clear-cut cases, but the more incorporeal the right, the more difficult it is to prove in a court of law. This is a case where evidentiary considerations and the possibility for abuse likely played a key role in the shaping of this right.

Consider the amount of money companies like Coca-Cola and Pepsi spend to produce extravagant commercials starring musicians like Britney Spears, Christina Aguilera, and CeeLo Green. Names such as Michael Jackson and, while not a musician, Cindy Crawford are icons in the world of successful advertising campaigns. In the third chapter, I mentioned a few lesser-known examples of such musicians, celebrities, and uses when I discussed the development of the right of publicity, but it is worth restating that this is not only an issue in the cases of the largest marketing campaigns with the biggest stars. Lesser known artists or smaller advertising campaigns such as Demi Lovato's music being used in commercials for Accuvue contact lenses and Ingrid Michaelson's having been used in commercials for home insurance are equally affected. One of my informants wrote the theme song to a television series on the Showtime network and two others have had their music used in local and regional commercials for everything from hospitals to McDonald's to the Detroit Zoo. This illustrates that there is not just a market for use of celebrities in association with advertising and marketing, but also for the use of local musicians.

My informants were not uniform in their attitudes toward uses of their music. Matt took a more opportunistic approach and was primarily interested in distribution of his music in whatever form it took. He told me he is, "typically just glad if anyone is hearing, ripping, downloading, remixing my music." (Interview, December 29, 2012) Ben explained that his main concern is, "that my work and I are treated with respect and fairness." (Interview, December 17,

2012) Norah expressed more concern about how uses of her music would affect her reputation. She told me that, "if it was hurting my image in any way or hurting people's perception of me, then I might not be so keen to that." (Interview, January 5, 2013) While these few responses span from ambivalence to concern over reputation, they show that there are certainly musicians who care about how uses of their music inform their identity. It might be argued that my first informant's attitude is primarily the result of his lack of experience with uses of his music that conflict with his morals or tarnish his identity. Either way, moral rights are every bit as much of a concern for musicians as they are for visual artists.

Moral rights, however, do not exist, either judicially or statutorily, in America to protect music. As I discussed earlier, Congress and American courts are reluctant to follow the lead of European courts and have been slow to consider adopting moral rights, so how do I arrive at the conclusion that such expansion is inevitable in the United States?

The first piece of evidence can be found in the evolution of the right of publicity. As I discussed earlier, the right of publicity has developed in three phases. In the first phase, the right of publicity attached when a celebrity's name, likeness, or something that can be readily identified as associated with that particular celebrity is used without that celebrity's authorization. In the second phase of right of publicity jurisprudence, the cause was essentially viewed as a form of unjust enrichment. During this phase, the cause of action was defined as "the right of an individual to control the commercial value of his name and likeness and to prevent their unauthorized exploitation by others." (Marx 1981, 487) The third phase of the evolution of the right of publicity developed as courts became more concerned with exploitation of personality, identity, voice, or ideology. In other words, the right of publicity has evolved from being about a celebrity's likeness to being about a celebrity's personality, beliefs, and reputation.

Of course, it does not necessarily follow that copyright law will evolve in the same manner that right of publicity law has. There are some factors suggesting that this migration has already begun to occur, though. First is the fact that copyright law with respect to the visual arts has already expanded to include "moral rights." Second is the fact that America has joined the Berne Convention, a body that already recognizes "moral rights" in its acceptance of European copyright law. Finally, that the courts have become more concerned with protecting identity, as evidenced by the development of right of publicity jurisprudence. As the understanding of the significance of identity and the field of identity studies becomes more important, so will the demand that the law protect the identity of not just visual artists, but musicians, authors, and anyone else currently protected under copyright law.

Phillip McIntyre has made the argument that music is naturally correlated to identity in his discussion of music and authenticity. He notes "that a band's 'credibility' also suffers once they enter what has been called 'the mainstream.'"(McIntyre 2012, 161) This is certainly evidence of a link between the band's music and their identity. Similarly, "Bob Dylan's authenticity depended on 'an assumption of the literary aesthetic code of the genius creator.' Dylan, when he famously swapped one style for another, from folk to rock, was vehemently rejected by his former folk audience." (169)[22] He suggests that, "in the very late 1960s rock performers in particular started to construct their authenticity around naturalness and the rejection of particular performance codes too closely identified with their parent's preferred performance styles." (168) Along the same lines, Joanna Demers suggests that, with the Copyright Act of 1976, *"the ink-and-paper composition is now viewed less as an expression and*

---

[22] Quoting Gamson, Joshua. 1994. *Claims to Fame: Celebrity in Contemporary America.* Berkeley, CA: University of California Press.

more as an idea… sound recordings are treated as expressions or manifestations of a compositional idea." (Demers 2006, 36)

I would suspect that, if you asked most musicians, they would agree that their music is a reflection of their identity. Choice of genre becomes almost as important as the clothes that a band wears or the subjects it sings about. Genres, and therefore musical sounds, reflect a certain ideology. It is not a far jump to see that musicians and, more importantly record companies, will ultimately demand that copyright law protect identity as well as product. In fact, Demers notes that "America's information and entertainment industries are entrenched in a fierce debate concerning the moral rights and economic incentive justifications for copyright." (Demers 2006, 13) So why do I think this change is inevitable?

If it were only one factor mitigating in favor of identity protection through statutory copyright law, it might be dismissed as inconsequential. Two might be more difficult to similarly dismiss. Three, though, constitutes a trend. I consider this evolution an imperative not only because I believe musicians will find such protection valuable, but because the law has already begun its slow but inevitable journey in that direction.

The fact of the matter is that copyright law has gradually been changing since 1989 to bring it more into conformity with international copyright law. These changes have come about because record companies (who are the real copyright holder in most cases) have demanded the greater protection that the Berne Convention affords them, but musicians have also raised their voices in the interest of protecting the one thing in the creative process that is still truly theirs: their identity. Recognition of moral rights is merely one more step along the way to that destination.

There can be no escaping the fact that copyright law is one of the most significant areas of the law to musicians and record companies. It is equally true that people typically think of piracy or copyright infringement when they think of copyright law. There is much more to it, though, and America is not too far behind the rest of the world in recognizing even more rights for musicians than simply protecting a collection of notes on a piece of paper.

Copyright protection has a long history, beginning in Europe and finding its way to America as early as the eighteenth century. Originally dealing with print materials and dealing with the right to copy those printed materials, copyright has expanded to cover all media of creative production, from books to music to visual art. While America is not yet in conformity with international law in all aspects of copyright law, it is slowly shifting toward that end. The most notable example of an area of divergence between American and international copyright law is the doctrine of moral rights.

Musicians have a rather large stage and can be very influential to their fans and followers. It is very simple for a musician to affect behavior and attitudes by presenting a certain image to the rest of the world. This image constitutes a portion of that musician's identity, or, as Turino would describe it, the collection of habits and attributes that the musician presents to the world. Due to that influence and its importance, both economically and ideologically, musicians would find it important to be able to control anything that might impact the public's perception and behavior with respect to that identity.

Moral rights would do just that. And while the doctrine has not yet found its way into American law for musicians, it does exist for visual artists and it is a well-accepted precept of copyright law in Canada and Europe. New York and California were on the cutting edge of incorporating this doctrine into their law with respect to visual artists. The federal government followed their lead in enacting legislation granting moral rights to visual artists on a national scale. The next logical step would be to extend that protection to anyone to whom copyright law currently applies.

Regardless of whether it is a good idea or not, it is inevitable that this change will occur. The winds of change are already shifting in that direction by way of this expansion for visual artists and the growing recognition of the importance of identity to the courts in the form of the right of publicity. America is also slowly falling in line with international notions of copyright law in conformity with the Berne Convention, so change is already occurring. This change will ultimately affect copyright law by introducing the concept of moral rights into American law.

CHAPTER V
THEORIZING THE IDEOLOGICAL VOICE

I have referred to the term "negative voice" several times throughout this thesis, but have not really explained what it is in much depth. Negative voice is a concept of my own creation that describes the use of voice without voice. In his discussion of Freud's drives, Mladen Dolar discusses the possibility of one using his "silence as a lever of his position, thus turning the silence into an act." (Dolar 2006, 158) This is the heart of the negative voice. We are faced with decisions every day and those decisions can often be essentialized and reduced to one of two choices: to do something or not to do something. While the use of binaries to describe distinct and specific concepts is problematic, there is a point at which they can be useful. Attention is generally focused on what we choose to do; yet little attention is paid to the road left untraveled. That road can be just as meaningful as the one we take.

So what is the negative voice and where does it come from? The negative voice is the ability to speak through the absence of speech. It is the right that any individual, and especially a celebrity, has to refuse to align himself with something as a means of protest or disassociation. The celebrity speaks volumes by not speaking at all, or by speaking in the negative. I start with the idea that actual speech or action is a positive act. I do not mean positive in the sense of it being a "good" thing, but more in the sense that action creates something: movement, products, capital, relationships, or anything else. In that sense, there is a net positive effect on production. By failing to act, then, we are creating a negative result. A use of voice is negative, then, when I have made my choice to not act expressly and specifically on ideological grounds.

The negative voice comes from the notion that your voice, in the ideological sense, is as much about what you do not say as it is about what you do say. Dolar discusses silence in the context of Ulysses' attempts to resist the Sirens when he explains that "the Sirens have a weapon far more effective than their voice: their silence, that is, the voice at its purest." (Dolar 2006, 171) Your identity is wrapped up in your general belief structure, so part of that identity entails what you do believe in, but also what you do not believe in. A musician has the right to be opposed to certain practices, hold people to certain ethical standards, and espouse a way of thinking or a way of life. The *Waits* case puts this into stark perspective because Waits had previously and publicly specifically spoken out against musicians doing endorsements in general, but the negative voice can exist on a smaller scale.

Bette Midler chose not to implicitly endorse Ford by choosing not to sing for their commercial. Perhaps it was because Ford did not offer her enough money, perhaps it was because she did not want to be associated with Ford, perhaps it was something else. Whatever her reasoning for rejecting Ford's offers, she exercised her negative voice by refusing their offer of affiliation. Perhaps, in light of these developments in the case law, *Sinatra* would be decided differently today. I believe that, at least in the Ninth Circuit, it would be. As a reflection of the musician's voice, his negative voice is equally as important as his physical voice.

Positive or Negative? How Do We Know?

At this point, it is important to go into a little more detail about the two types of voices I have mentioned in this chapter: positive and negative. To the best of my knowledge, voice has not been theorized in this manner before, so this is fairly uncharted territory. As a result, I focus primarily on my own ideas along with the results of my fieldwork in order to construct a method

of theorizing ideological voice that can be instructive for voice studies in general.

When Do We Use Our Ideological Voice?

In a sense, we use our ideological voice every minute of every day. Broadly conceived,

every decision we make reflects our ideas, beliefs, and ethics. Such a broad conception is

essentially useless because it obviates the need to even consider the ideological voice. A concept

must not only include, but also exclude, or it loses its meaning. I recall discussions with other

music scholars in my own life about how to define music. As Bach and Beethoven gave way to

Schonberg and Berg, then to John Cage, we expanded our conception of what music is. But

should our definition include sounds occurring in nature? How about the sounds of the hermit

thrush, which have definite and complex musical qualities? Or the mating call of a wolf? Even

whale songs or dolphins chattering have a communicative quality to them and certainly an

intentionality that could be thought of as musical. But then, extending our conception, we can

think about the sound of wind blowing against wind chimes or the rain on a tin roof. At what

point does music stop and mere sound begin? If there is no point of demarcation, then it becomes

useless to even have "music" as a term because everything is music.

I do not bring this up to propose a definition of music, but rather to illustrate a point

about the dangers of overly broad conceptions of terminology. It is, therefore, necessary to place

limits around the idea of ideological voice so that we can more meaningfully consider the ideas

of positive and negative voice. While it is true that we are almost constantly using our

ideological voices in some sense, such a broad conception of the term swallows itself and becomes useless. The first limitation should be that use of ideological voice should reflect a conscious decision. While the subconscious certainly reflects our deep-seated beliefs, there should be a component of intentionality in order to separate conscious decisions from mere instinctive ones. Even intentionality, though, is not a term without its complexities.

There are three levels of intentionality. The first level would be the unintentional, or instinctive. We might also consider acts of subsistence or survival within this group. An example in this category might be eating. Eating is a biological imperative. It is not instinctive in the sense that, unlike breathing, we must choose to eat and we can forego food for any number of reasons. It is necessary for survival, though, and, after acknowledging the necessity of the act itself, contains potential layers of meaning. The second level would be the first of those layers and it would include generalized decisions focused on the act itself. An example of this type of decision would be vegetarianism. I might choose to forego any meat for ideological or health reasons (whether they be valid or not). This would reflect an ideological position based upon the act of eating itself that reflects a certain belief. An example of decisions on this level that might have lesser implications with respect to ideological voice might include basing decisions upon taste preference. On the third level, though, I may also make decisions about eating that are not centered on the act itself, but by which my decisions relative to the act reflect an ideological stance about something extrinsic to consumption. This extrinsic ideology might include patronizing a restaurant that donates a portion of its proceeds to a particular charity or one that supports a particular cause.

With respect to the ideological voice, each of these three levels of intentionality reflects an increasing potential presence of ideological voice. The first level of instinctive acts possesses only a minor possible reflection of ideological voice, if any at all. The second level of intentionality has greater potential to reflect ideological voice in a meaningful way because it deals with conscious decisions about things that may or may not reflect ideology. This level can be conceived of as a reflection of positive or negative voice. The greatest level of potential reflection of ideological voice, however, must be in that third level of intentionality. In a sense, it is almost a necessity that this level reflects the most significant and meaningful use of ideological voice because it is, by definition, based almost entirely on a decision about something other than the ostensible act itself. It is this third level upon which I would like to focus.

As I noted in the Introduction, it is also helpful to contemplate the ideological voice in a manner similar to the aural voice. When considering the aural voice, you may consider the actual sound, the meaning of the sound, and the mechanisms that produce the sound. Similarly, for the ideological voice you can consider the action that someone takes, the ideological position that action represents, and the mechanism that enables that action. So, for example, with Tom Waits, his actions were to speak out against endorsements and to refuse to do any. The ideological position that action represents would be his belief that doing endorsements is selling out and that it compromises artistic integrity. The mechanisms that enable that action would include utilizing the legal system to protect his ideological position or that his celebrity status provides him with a podium upon which to communicate that position to a wide audience. This is the foundation of the discursive theory of ideological voice.

Distinguishing the Positive from the Negative

Returning to the eating analogy, we can now distinguish between positive and negative voice and equate them to ideology in a meaningful way for voice studies. Quite simply, positive voice is when you choose a particular path in order to make a statement, while negative voice is when you avoid a particular path in order to make a statement. For example, I would be using my positive voice if I chose to eat at a restaurant that supported marriage equality while I would be using my negative voice if I chose to avoid a restaurant that opposed marriage equality. This reflects upon voice because both are ways in which I would be using my actions to reflect my voice in an ideological sense.

For musicians, there are many ways in which they can utilize their ideological voice. Bono from U2 has been known to use the platform of his concert stage in order to promote causes that he is involved in. I was at a U2 concert in the mid-2000s where he encouraged audience members to take out their cell phones and text their name to a certain number to demonstrate their support for his One Campaign. Names would then flash across a giant video monitor, but every audience member who texted their name was then signed up to receive mass text messages from the One Campaign (standard text messaging rates apply, of course). The use of positive voice does not have to be so explicit, though. Positive voice can also be implicit, both actually and perceived.

In an actual sense, a musician may be promoting or endorsing a cause by letting his music be used by that organization or by appearing as a spokesperson. One of the reasons companies hire celebrities, though, is because they hope that the general public will then assume that the celebrity endorses that product or organization. In fact, the best possible outcome would be for the public to associate that celebrity with the organization. This is where advertisers and marketers harness the power of the cultural cohort to drive commerce and take advantage of the perceived implicit positive voice. I say that this is a perceived use of implicit positive voice because the musician may not have an opinion about the company or organization and may simply be collecting a paycheck. This drives at the heart of why Tom Waits likely opposes musicians endorsing products.

Unfortunately, despite my best efforts, I was unable to obtain my own interview with Mr. Waits, but there have been several interviews with Mr. Waits in which he discussed his stance on commercials. In a letter that Waits apparently wrote in response to a story in the magazine *The Nation* regarding The Doors' drummer John Densmore refusing to do commercials, Waits said that "artists who take money for ads poison and pervert their songs. It reduces them to the level of a jingle, a word that describes the sound of change in your pocket, which is what your songs become. Remember, when you sell your songs for commercials, you are selling your audience as well." (Waits 2002) Waits referenced his identity in a New York Times article from 2006 about subsequent legal battles with advertisers over sound-alikes when he noted that "it's part of an artist's odyssey… discovering your own voice and finding the combination of qualities that makes you unique. It's kind of like your face, your identity. Now I've got these evil doppelgangers out there – my evil twin who is undermining every move I make." (Sisario 2006, E3) His aversion to advertising stems, in part, to his reaction to the only time he ever did a commercial about 10 years prior to the Frito Lay case. He noted that he was down on his luck and needed the money, but after, he felt artistically like "artistically, I had sold myself down the river. I felt I had betrayed something in me." (United 1990) As Waits himself pointed out in the Frito Lay case, the fact that people thought he was singing for a commercial made him look like a hypocrite because of this implicit positive voice. Advertisers are taking advantage of this implicit positive association with their product in order to drive sales. Waits believes that "your credibility, your integrity and your honor are things no company should be able to buy." (Waits 2002)

Advertising may also be used to help expose musicians to the public and drive musical success. One of the most striking examples of this phenomenon is Moby. He licensed all 18 tracks on his album *Play* for use in advertising in 2000. Prior to this, he was relatively unknown, but his licensing agreements "led to radio airplay that almost certainly would not have been conceivable otherwise, and record sales in the millions." (Klein 2009, 59) Moby's tremendous success "validated advertising as a launching pad for lesser-known or new musicians in both the independent and major label music worlds, where suddenly licensing became seen as not simply an extra source of revenue, but a way to break an artist." (59)

It is interesting to note that, in my formulation of voice, it is not only possible to use negative and positive voice concurrently, but it is almost necessary. If I were to choose not to endorse a particular product it could, as with Tom Waits, be because I specifically want to distance myself from that particular product or endorsements in general. It could also be because they aren't paying me enough money, that I promised that song to someone else, or any number of other possible reasons. When I have utilized my positive voice to speak out on a particular issue, though, then my use of negative voice through disassociation relative to that issue becomes more explicit and identifiable for what it is. The thing that separates silence from negative voice is its association with something else, presumably a use of the positive voice.

Some of my informants reinforced these ideas in my interviews with them. Tom acknowledged that, "identity and reputation are everything in this business," underscoring the importance of artistic integrity and credibility. (Interview, December 19, 2012) Sarah explained that, "an image is a big thing. It is. As much as I don't like to admit that, it just is. And you see it as soon as you're in the scene." (Interview, November 10, 2012) While none of my informants were as adamantly opposed to endorsement as Waits is, they all expressed a concern about their music or voice being used to endorse products that they did not believe in. Sarah further explained that, "when I started singing professionally, I made a promise that I would never do anything that was not genuine. So I would never become something, be something, sing something, wear something that was not me. And I would never put on a mask." (Interview, November 10, 2012) As it relates to endorsement, she stated that, "I've gotta like the product and it's gotta genuinely reflect who I am." (Interview, November 10, 2012) Will summed up my contention regarding negative voice succinctly when he told me, "if you don't want to get involved, just keep quiet." (Interview, January 5, 2013)

This idea is not without its problems, though. To a certain extent, every "famous" musician has been commodified. One common criticism of independent bands with cult underground followings that later sign major record deals is that they are "selling out." This implies a type of caving to commercial influence that bears some similarity to Waits' position on endorsements. Is Tom Waits, therefore, a hypocrite because he accepts large amounts of money from record companies and movie producers to sing or act in projects with wide commercial appeal or is there a difference? Matt addressed this apparent conflict by telling me, "I think the concept of paying someone for their art, to use their art, to borrow their art, to whatever, is a good concept. I think it needs to be that way." (Interview, December 29, 2012) The overriding issue, then, becomes your conception of the term "art" and how that applies, if at all, to the work that a musician is doing.

I do not believe the answer to the question of whether Waits is already a hypocrite by participating in the commercial aspect of the music industry is so simple as to be capable of being theorized here. As with Tom Waits and the use of negative voice, though, it really boils down to personal opinion. My role here is not to valuate commercialism or different genres of music, but rather to explore how voice is manifested and communicated by musicians and how voice ties into and reflects personal identity. The works I have referenced in this thesis make a case for the ideas of positive and negative voice and my field interviews support the notion that these are concepts that come into play for musicians, both consciously and subconsciously, when considering and crafting their own identities.

As you can see, though, distinguishing between positive and negative voice is not so clear-cut because there is usually some degree of overlap along with some measure of uncertainty or ambiguity as to whether negative voice is even being used at all. On one hand, Dolar reminds us that "not all voices are heard, and perhaps the most intrusive and compelling are the unheard voice, and the most deafening thing can be silence." (Dolar 2006, 14) It is true that silence can speak volumes, but it can also say nothing at all. It is important to consider the negative voice as a powerful reflection of identity and ideology, though, because there can be no doubt that it functions in that way. The negative voice, in a sense, is similar to the idea of opportunity cost in economic theory. Opportunity cost would be the value of forgone opportunities where negative voice would equate to the value of actually forgoing those opportunities. Negative voice, then, becomes a powerful tool that musicians can use to reflect their identity to their cultural cohorts and craft their image in a way that best supports their personal ideologies.

CHAPTER VI
CONCLUSION

I began this thesis by asking what defines a musician. Over the ensuing pages I have answered that question, as well as provided some insight as to why it should matter to scholars, to musicians, and to the public at large. The legal system, through legislation and the judiciary, has instituted a means of redress if musicians have been harmed in any number of ways. The most widely known of these means is copyright law, but copyright law, in practice, does not really protect musicians. What, then, do musicians hope to protect and how can the law provide that protection? Those are the questions that are central to this thesis.

I began my thesis by discussing identity in general. Identity is a difficult concept to define with respect to musicians because of the unique place they hold in society and the many layers of identity that exist simultaneously for most musicians. On one hand, there is individual identity, which Turino thinks of as the way in which an individual represents himself to himself and to others. Turino's definition is actually more convoluted than that, but what he was trying to do is to contemplate all of the conceivable formulations of how an individual and others could interact with respect to the individual's habits and attributes. He further considered the ways in which that identity interacts with the social environment: how it influences the social environment and how it, in turn, is informed by the social environment.

Individual identity is further problematic because of the many simultaneous identities that an individual possesses, all of which interact with the social environment in different ways, in different spheres, and on different levels. I also proposed the ideas of "true" and "perceived" identity and discussed some of the difficulties of those ideas. The idea that there can be a "true" you implies that there is something that is objective and verifiable, which is problematic in and of itself. Identity, then, is really more about perception than objectively verifiable fact. Even as it pertains to identity of the self, there are layers of "real" and "perceived" operating in dialectical ways that make identifying a true identity effectively impossible. Identity is self-validating, though, in that the instant that we conceive of ourselves in a certain way and act in accordance, that becomes a part of the reality of who we are and what our identity is. Our actions take the perceived and make it real.

Individual identity is only part of the equation, though. Collective identity is also a presence in the complicated web of the dialectical relationship between identity and the social environment. Collective identity involves similarities that function as a unifying theme, if you will, for a group. These groups function as cultural or identity cohorts, as Turino would describe them. Individuals thought of as leaders by members of these cohorts, then, have something of a trickle-down effect on both the collective and individual identities of cohort members in all of their complex manifestations, which then influence culture. This is why musicians are so significant.

They act as focal points for cultural and identity cohorts and it is through the use of their voice, in both the physical and ideological sense, that they effectuate a profound influence on society. This whole discussion, then, is really mainly about negotiations of power and influence through the use of voice.

I then discussed voice as a theoretical construct. While voice can be thought of as the physical apparatus that creates sound (a construction of voice that musicians certainly do use), it can also be thought of as the message as well as the medium. Beyond just being the message and the means by which it is communicated, voice can also be thought of as a marker for credibility and sincerity. Therefore, voice includes a physical production, an ideological belief, and a marker of credibility, making it one of the most powerful influences on creation and shaping of identity, both individual and collective, and negotiations of power amongst and within collectives.

After discussing identity, I moved into a discussion of copyright law in America in general. Copyright is usually thought of as a means of protecting musicians from having their music stolen by other people. While this is certainly true, it is also a very basic conception of copyright and fails to address many nuances and polemics surrounding copyright law. First, I discussed the historical development of copyright law beginning with its origins in Europe and extending into modern copyright law in America. Copyright was originally conceived of as a means of protecting the right of publishers to copy written works (their right to copy, or copyright). The first legislative enactment establishing copyright was the Statute of Anne in England, which established the right to copy new written works for 14 years (21 years for existing works). The purpose behind copyright was to promote creativity while still allowing subsequent authors to utilize existing works to create their own derivative works. It was therefore important not just to establish exclusive rights to copy works, but also to limit those rights in duration.

In America, the first copyright statute was the Copyright Act of 1790, which was based largely upon the Statute of Anne. This statute remained in effect until the Copyright Act of 1909, which was spurred by the need for copyright law to keep pace with developments in technology. This statute covered not just written works, but any creative works (including music). Coverage under the act lasted for 28 years with the ability to renew the right for an additional 28 years. This law was eventually replaced by the Copyright Act of 1976, which is the law that is currently in effect today. Currently, the length of copyright protection extends for the life of the author plus 70 years for new works and a fixed 28 years with a 67-year renewal for existing works that were under protection at the time the 1976 act took effect. This gradual prolongation from 14 years to life + 70 years is believed to be the result of lobbying efforts from the major corporations holding exclusive rights under copyright law, not the actual authors of the works protected by the law. Critics of current copyright law believe that it primarily benefits major corporations and stifles creative development.

As a result of this belief, some musicians have utilized emerging technologies to circumvent record companies altogether and avoid copyright protection. Radiohead is the most vocal and successful example of this model, but the DIY record industry has evolved to allow musicians to create their own recordings and crowdsource their marketing to provide a more cost-effective means of publicity and distribution while retaining all copyrights for themselves. Additional developments, such as Creative Commons, permits authors to make their works available to others for free use for whatever purposes the author chooses (see, for example, the Frontispiece of this thesis). While major record companies are still the power players in the music production business, these developments have been slowly growing in popularity and having an impact on the major labels.

This all ties back into identity because of the ways in which economic interests and music production relate in a dialectical manner with identity. As the power of major recording labels has increased, so has their power over musicians and the extent of their benefits under copyright law. Concurrently, though, they are currently being assailed by a monster of their own creation. Record labels have been so effective at marketing musicians through their identities that the musicians have amassed the cultural cache to influence their cohorts and society in general. The economic interest in production has shifted from one of the tangible product to the identity. Musicians are now finding a way to parlay that cultural influence into alternative means of production and distribution that leave the record company out of the loop and enable musicians to reclaim control of their own creations on an increasing basis. We are still a long way from a major shift in the power dynamic between record company and musician, but the balance in that power dynamic is slowly shifting.

I then discussed the right of publicity, a judicial creation that is often conflated with copyright, but which stands alone as distinct from copyright law. The right of publicity was initially conceived of as a way of protecting visual likenesses, but has evolved to encompass identity. It has evolved in three phases and I discussed those phases and theorized them as a natural evolution rather than a disconnected departure. One of the foundational concerns with respect to the right of publicity has as much to do with misleading the public and deception as it does with fair compensation for celebrities.

In the first phase of the right of publicity, courts were concerned with visual representations. For example, in a case involving late night talk show host Johnny Carson, a portable toilet company had used the famous catch-phrase "Here's Johnny" in its advertisement and Carson sued for right of publicity. The court mentioned identity when rendering its decision, but basically the court was considering something fairly tangible, a phrase in this case. The court's decision was based upon Carson's pecuniary interest in this reflection of his identity and the fact that he was not compensated for it. Another example that I did not discuss earlier involved a racecar driver who had a distinct vehicle with a unique configuration of decals and decorations upon it. A company utilized an image of the car, but removed the number from the car and anything containing the driver's name and used that image in its advertisements. Again, this was a fairly tangible representation that was strongly associated with the driver and the court ruled that the company was taking advantage of his fame without properly compensating him. The first phase of the right of publicity could then be summarized as protecting tangible representations of celebrities from being used without proper compensation. At this point, the primary concern was economic.

In the 1980s, the right of publicity entered its second phase where courts began to concern themselves with more intangible interests. One illustrative case representing this development involved the Marx Brothers, who sued a production company that produced a play where the actors simulated the unique styles of the Marx Brothers. In the *Marx* case, the court recognized the importance of celebrities in the personas they capitalize upon as representations to the public. The second phase is most noteworthy because courts began thinking of a musician's persona as something tangible, much as they had considered things like a baseball player's likeness or the unique placement of decals on a racecar driver's car tangible. The *Marx* case is also noteworthy because it brings the idea of celebrity impersonators into question. If the defendants in the *Marx* case cannot have their actors imitate the unique performance styles of the Marx Brothers, how then can celebrity impersonators get away with what they do? Essentially, the determining factor is intent. If the intent is to deceive the public and capitalize upon that deception, the right of publicity comes into play. If the intent is parody, then the First Amendment applies and the representation is protected.

There are two cases that exemplify the developments of the third phase of the development of the right of publicity. The first involved Bette Midler in a case where Midler sued Ford Motor Company because they hired a Bette Midler sound-alike to sing one of Midler's famous songs for a commercial after first approaching and being denied by Midler to appear in the commercial herself. The court acknowledged the connection between physical voice and identity in finding that this violation of Midler's very identity constituted grounds for a lawsuit. This was the first time a court explicitly held that co-opting a musician's identity alone was sufficient to support a right of publicity claim.

The second and, arguably, more significant case involved Tom Waits. Waits was staunchly opposed to musicians endorsing any products at all, so when he was approached by Frito Lay to sing a parody of one of his own songs, he naturally refused. Much as Ford did with Midler, Frito Lay then hired a sound-alike to sing the song for the commercial. Waits sued not only on pecuniary grounds, but also on ideological grounds. He claimed that listeners might think that he was actually singing in the commercial and, his stance on musician endorsements being a well-known part of his identity, might question his integrity and credibility. The court not only upheld the right of publicity claim, but also upheld an award for mental distress based upon Waits' shock, anger, and embarrassment. This represents the final development in the right of publicity and brings us up to today where musicians now enjoy significant protection of their identity through judicial doctrine, but not statute.

This is not to say that there are no statutory means of protecting identity, both at home and abroad. After examining the right of publicity, a judicial creation, I went on to consider the moral rights doctrine, a legislative one. The moral rights doctrine primarily exists in international copyright law (including the Berne Convention) and protects an author's moral claim to how his creation is used. While this law has had purchase in international copyright law for over a century, it has gained very little traction in America. Currently, the only type of creation protected by the moral rights doctrine is visual art. New York and California both have statutes protecting visual art under the moral rights doctrine and these statutes prompted Congress to pass the Visual Artists Rights Act of 1990, which granted moral rights to visual artists on a national level.

While there is no guarantee that moral rights will ever be granted to musicians, I examined some reason why that might be on the horizon in America. The first reason I cited was the evolution of the right of publicity. As I explained, the right of publicity has gradually evolved from protection of a tangible representation, such as a photograph or a distinctive design, into a protection of identity and even integrity. The second reason is the enactment of moral rights legislation in New York, California, and in federal law protecting visual artists. This demonstrates that lawmakers are aware of the importance of protecting an artist's integrity and the very real danger that their integrity will be exploited without sufficient compensation. This danger is no less present with musicians as it is for visual artists, so it only goes to follow that moral rights will eventually be extended to all forms of creative production just as copyright was extended from print materials to music and other forms of creative production. Finally, there is the fact that America has now joined the Berne Convention, a set of international rules aimed at providing an international framework for copyright enforcement across national borders.

Economic interests for musicians have shifted from their creative product to their persona and identity and the law is adapting in recognition of that shift. Case law has already evolved to account for that development, but legislation has been slow to follow suit, as legislation often is. There are enough high profile musicians and celebrities now drawing attention to this deficiency that lawmakers are becoming aware of the issue and are beginning to address it. This represents a fundamental shift in the rights of musicians and has tremendous implications for the creation of new music because of the swing in the balance of power between musicians and record companies. Until that shifting environment begins to settle down and work itself out, the primary economic interest of most musicians rests in their identity and ideology.

The final chapter of this thesis explored the way in which musicians use their voice as a reflection of their ideology. In theorizing the ideological voice, I introduced the concepts of the positive and negative voice. This distinction is important because what we choose to not do can often be as telling as what we choose to do. We use our positive voice when we choose an affirmative course of action that reflects our ideology in some manner. By affirmative course of action, I mean that we choose to act in a manner reflective of that ideology. The negative voice is the exact opposite. It comes into play when we choose to forego action because of an ideological stance.

The use of negative voice is most clearly illustrated in the cases involving Bette Midler and Tom Waits. For whatever reason, whether it be economic or moral, they chose not to endorse certain products. When those companies acted in a manner that might mislead people into believing they had endorsed those products, it not only misled the public but it assailed their right of disassociation. While the motivation for Midler's refusal to endorse Ford is unclear, there is no such ambiguity in the case of Tom Waits. He had been quite vocal and outspoken in his beliefs about artistic integrity as it relates to product endorsement. Frito Lay's use of a Tom Waits sound-alike not only infringed upon his right to control the use of his physical voice, but also attacked his integrity within his cultural cohort and within society at large. His integrity was so clearly attacked that it warranted an award of not just compensatory damages, but also of emotional distress.

While it is certainly possible to conceive of instances where positive or negative voice exist alone, they are most effective when used together. If Tom Waits had not vocally spoken out against musician endorsements, his contention that Frito Lay had damaged his integrity within his cultural cohort would be less effective than it was because of his use of positive voice. In a sense, it is almost the use of positive voice that enables the recognition and use of negative voice. The interplay of these representations of ideology is crucial to protecting a musician's economic interests in their identity.

Identity is of prime importance to musicians and has become one of the most significant economic interests that they possess. It is carefully and consciously crafted and has a strong influence on society at large. Musicians go to great lengths to conceive of and cultivate those identities, which are fluid and ever-evolving things. Since copyright law has evolved to act as more of a protection for the economic interests of big business and less of the economic interests of musicians, the law has responded by adapting to provide those protections to musicians. It has done so through the development and evolution of the right of publicity and through the moral rights doctrine.

I have attempted to provide a new means of considering voice from an ideological perspective by marrying already existing ideas from a number of sources with my own concepts with respect to ideological voice. In doing so, I have created a new theoretical framework for future studies of ideological voice that can inform future voice studies. Musicians have a tendency to focus on their physical body because that is what actually creates their product. As a physical manifestation, it naturally becomes a convenient focal point, but it is not the only thing that musicians should be conscious of or concerned about. In today's creative environment, a musician's greatest asset is not talent, but his identity. Drawing attention to this shift in economic interest enables scholars to more effectively theorize it and musicians to better protect it.

I began this thesis by asking what defines a musician. While I have answered that question in a meaningful way, it is only a starting point. This is in part because it is a very difficult question with an answer that is as complex as you are willing to make it, but also because it is something variable and ever-changing. The theoretical framework I have developed here can serve as a starting point for theorizing that question and developing more meaningful answers to it that shed a brighter light on the ideological voice and what it means to musicians. It is that process that enables musicians to better explore and develop their identities and for ethnomusicologists to better understand how that informs their work.

BIBLIOGRAPHY

Books and Articles

Alvarez, Alfredo. 2004. *The Writer's Voice*. New York, NY: W.W. Norton & Co.

Auslander, Philip. 1999. *Liveness: Performance in a Mediatized Culture*. New York, NY:
Routledge.

Barthes, Roland. 1977. "The Grain of the Voice." In *Image, Music, Text*, Translated by Stephen
Heath, 179-189. New York, NY: Noonday Press.

Bernstein, Mary. 2005. "Identity Politics." *Annual Review of Sociology* 31: 47-74.

Blacking, John. 1973. *How Musical is Man?* Seattle, WA: University of Washington Press.

Cavarero, Adriana. 2005. *For More Than One Voice: Toward a Philosophy of Vocal Expression*.
Stanford, CA: Stanford University Press.

Cerulo, Karen A. 1997. "Identity Construction: New Issues, New Directions," *Annual Review of
Sociology* 23: 385-409.

Chiou, Jyh-Shen, Chien-yi Huang and Hsin-hui Lee. 2005. "The Antecedents of Music Piracy
Attitudes and Intentions." *Journal of Business Ethics* 57(2): 161-174.

Demers, Joanna. 2006. *Steal This Music: How Intellectual Property Law Affects Musical
Creativity*. Athens, GA: University of Georgia Press.

Dolar, Mladen. 2006. *A Voice and Nothing More*. Cambridge, MA: MIT Press.

Duncan, Lauren E. and Abigail J. Stewart. 2007. "Personal Political Salience: The Role of
Personality in Collective Identity and Action." *Political Psychology* 28(2): 143-164

Easley, Robert F. 2005. "Ethical Issues in the Music Industry Response to Innovation and
Piracy." *Journal of Business Ethics* 62(2): 163-168.

Frith, Simon. 1996. *Performing Rites: On the Value of Popular Music*. Cambridge, MA: Harvard
    University Press.

Frith, Simon and Lee Marshall. 2004. "Making Sense of Copyright." In *Music and Copyright*, 1-
    21. New York, NY: Routledge.

Future of Music Coalition Artist Revenue Streams. 2014. "42 Revenue Streams." Future of
    Music Coalition. Accessed March 8. http://money.futureofmusic.org/40-revenue-streams/

Gamson, Joshua. 1994. *Claims to Fame: Celebrity in Contemporary America*. Berkeley, CA:
    University of California Press.

Hart, Henry M., Jr. and Albert M. Sacks. 1994. *The Legal Process: Basic Problems in the
    Making and Application of Law*. Westbury, NY: The Foundation Press.

Hilderbrand, Lucas. 2007. "Youtube: Where Cultural Memory and Copyright Converge." *Film
    Quarterly* 61(1): 48-57.

Ihde, Don. 1976. *Listening and Voice: Phenomenologies of Sound*. Albany, NY: SUNY Press.

Klein, Bethany. 2009. *As Heard on TV: Popular Music in Advertising*. Burlington, VT: Ashgate
    Publishing Company.

Klein, Jeff. Forthcoming. "Tom Waits and the Right of Publicity: Protecting the Artist's
    Negative Voice." *Popular Music and Society*.

Kleine, Robert E., III, Susan Schultz Kleine and Jerome B. Kernan. 1993. "Mundane
    Consumption and the Self: A Social-Identity Perspective." *Journal of Consumer
    Psychology* 2(3): 209-235.

Kretschmer, Martin and Friedmann Kawohl. 2004. "The History and Philosophy of Copyright."
    In *Music and Copyright*, 21-53. New York, NY: Routledge.

Ku, Raymond Shih Ray. 2002. "The Creative Destruction of Copyright: Napster and the New Economics of Digital Technology." *The University of Chicago Law Review* 69(1): 263-324.

McEwen, Richard. 1994. "The Frito Bandito's Last Stand: *Waits* Rocks Performers' Rights Into the Media Age." *Journal of Law and Commerce* 14: 123-140.

McLeod, Kembrew. 2005. *Freedom of Expression®: Overzealous Copyright Bozos and Other Enemies of Creativity*. New York: Doubleday.

McLeod, Kembrew and Peter DiCola. 2011. *Creative License: The Law and Culture of Digital Sampling*. Durham, NC: Duke University Press.

McIntyre, Phillip. 2012. *Creativity and Cultural Production: Issues for Media Practice*. New York, NY: Palgrave MacMillan.

Meizel, Katherine. 2011a. "Hearing Voices: Toward a Model for the Study of Vocality." Society for Ethnomusicology. Philadelphia Sheraton Downtown Hotel, Philadelphia, PA. 18, November. Conference Paper.

_____. 2011b. *Idolized: Music, Media, and Identity in American Idol*. Bloomington, IN: Indiana University Press.

Moser, David J. and Cheryl L. Slay. 2012. *Music Copyright Law*. Boston, MA: Cengage Learning.

Myers, Fred. 2004. "Ontologies of the Image and Economics of Exchange." *American Ethnologist* 31(1): 5-20.

Nimmer, Melville B., Paul Marcus, David A. Myers, and David Nimmer. 2006. *Cases and Materials on Copyright and Other Aspects of Entertainment Litigation Including Unfair Competition, Defamation, Privacy*. Newark, NJ: LexisNexis.

Padden, Carol & Tom L. Humphries. 2006. *Inside Deaf Culture*. Cambridge, MA: Harvard

    University Press.

Prosser, Dean. 1960. "Privacy." *California Law Review* 48: 383-423.

Restatement (Third) of Unfair Competition (1993).

Schlichter, Annette. 2011. "Do Voices Matter? Vocality, Materiality, and Gender Performance."

    Body & Society 17(1): 31-52.

Scollon, Ron. 1995. "Plagiarism and Ideology: Identity in Intercultural Discourse." *Language in*

    Society 24(1): 1-28.

Seeger, Anthony. 1992. "Ethnomusicology and Music Law." *Ethnomusicology* 36(3): 345-359.

Sisario, Ben. 2006. "Still Fighting For the Right to his Voice." *New York Times*. January 20: E3.

Sprigman, Christopher. 2004. "Reform(aliz)ing Copyright." *Stanford Law Review* 57(2): 485-

    568.

Stahl, Matt. 2012. *Unfree Masters: Popular Music and the Politics of Work (Refiguring*

    American Music).

Stamets, Russell A. 1994. "Ain't Nothing Like the Real Thing, Baby: The Right of Publicity and

    the Singing Voice." *Federal Communications Law Journal* 56(2): 347-372.

Stim, Rich. 2003. *Music Law: How to Run Your Band's Business*. Berkley, CA: NOLO.

Turino, Thomas. 1999. "Sign of Imagination, identity, and Experience: A Peircian Semiotic

    Theory for Music." *Ethnomusicology*, 43, (2): 221-255.

_____. 2008. *Music as Social Life: The Politics of Participation*. Chicago, IL: University of

    Chicago Press.

United Press International. 1990. "Tom Waits Sues Frito Lay, Says His Voice appropriated."

    April 13. *Los Angeles Times*. Accessed March 9, 2014. http://articles.latimes.com/1990-

    04-13/business/fi-1428_1_singer-tom-waits

Waits, Tom. 2002. Letter to the editor, *The Nation*, October 7.

Wallach, Jeremy. 2008. *Modern Noise, Fluid Genres*. Madison, WI: The University of

    Wisconsin Press.

Weinreb, Lloyd L. 1998. "Copyright for Functional Expression." *Harvard Law Review* 111(5):

    1149-1254.

Weintraub, Andrew. 2009. Introduction to *Music and Cultural Rights*, by Andrew Weintraub and

    Bell Yung, 1-18. Chicago, IL: University of Illinois Press.

Weintraub, Andrew and Bell Yung. 2009. *Music and Cultural Rights*. Chicago, IL: University of

    Illinois Press.

Wu, Timothy. 2004. "Copyright's Communications Policy." *Michigan Law Review* 103(2): 278-

    366.

Young, Miriama. 2006. "Latent Body – Plastic, Malleable, Inscribed: The Human Voice, the

    Body and the Sound of its Transformation Through Technology." *Contemporary Music*

    Review 25(1-1): 81-92.

Cases and Statutes

15 USC §1501, *et seq.*

17 USC §1, *et seq.*

Bear Foot, Inc. v. Chandler, 965 S.W.2d 386, 389 (Mo. App. 1998)

California Civil Code, Section 987

Carson v. Here's Johnny Portable Toilets, Inc., 698 F.2d 831 (6th Cir. 1983)

Feagre & Benson, LLP v. Purdy, 367 F.2d 1238 (D. Minn. 2005)

Groucho Marx Productions, Inc. v. Day and Night Company, Inc., 523 F.Supp 485 (SD NY
    1981)

Haelan Laboratories, Inc. v. Topps Chewing Gum, Inc., 202 F.2d 866 (2nd Cir. 1953)

Jim Henson Productions, Inc. v. John T. Brady & Associates, Inc., 867 F.Supp 175 (SD NY
    1994)

Midler v. Ford Motor Company, 849 F.2d 460 (9th Cir. 1988).

Prima v. Darden Restaurants, Inc., 78 F.Supp.2d 337, 350 (USDC NJ 2000)

Sinatra v. The Goodyear Tire & Rubber Co., 435 F.2d 711 (9th Cir. 1970)

Title C, Articles 11-14, New York Arts & Cult. Aff. Law

Visual Artists Rights Act, 104 Stat. 5128 (1990)

Waits v. Frito-Lay, Inc., 978 F.2d 1093 (9th Cir. 1992).

White v. Samsung Electronics America, Inc., 971 F.2d 1395 (1992).

APPENDIX 1 – HSRB APPROVAL LETTER

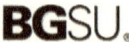

BOWLING GREEN STATE UNIVERSITY
Office of Research Compliance

DATE: August 21, 2012

TO: Jeff Klein, MM
FROM: Bowling Green State University Human Subjects Review Board

PROJECT TITLE: [338948-3] The Right of Publicity: A Study of the Artist's Negative Voice
SUBMISSION TYPE: Revision

ACTION: APPROVED
APPROVAL DATE: August 20, 2012
EXPIRATION DATE: July 18, 2013
REVIEW TYPE: Expedited Review

REVIEW CATEGORY: Expedited review category # 7

Thank you for your submission of Revision materials for this project. The Bowling Green State University Human Subjects Review Board has APPROVED your submission. This approval is based on an appropriate risk/benefit ratio and a project design wherein the risks have been minimized. All research must be conducted in accordance with this approved submission.

The final approved version of the consent document(s) is available as a published Board Document in the Review Details page. You must use the approved version of the consent document when obtaining consent from participants. Informed consent must continue throughout the project via a dialogue between the researcher and research participant. Federal regulations require that each participant receives a copy of the consent document.

Please note that you are responsible to conduct the study as approved by the HSRB. If you seek to make any changes in your project activities or procedures, those modifications must be approved by this committee prior to initiation. Please use the modification request form for this procedure.

You have been approved to enroll *10-15* participants. If you wish to enroll additional participants you must seek approval from the HSRB.

All UNANTICIPATED PROBLEMS involving risks to subjects or others and SERIOUS and UNEXPECTED adverse events must be reported promptly to this office. All NON-COMPLIANCE issues or COMPLAINTS regarding this project must also be reported promptly to this office.

This approval expires on July 18, 2013. You will receive a continuing review notice before your project expires. If you wish to continue your work after the expiration date, your documentation for continuing review must be received with sufficient time for review and continued approval before the expiration date.

Good luck with your work. If you have any questions, please contact the Office of Research Compliance at 419-372-7716 or hsrb@bgsu.edu. Please include your project title and reference number in all correspondence regarding this project.

This letter has been electronically signed in accordance with all applicable regulations, and a copy is retained within Bowling Green State University Human Subjects Review Board's records.

APPENDIX 2 – HSRB MODIFICATION APPROVAL LETTER

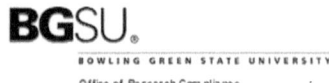

BOWLING GREEN STATE UNIVERSITY
Office of Research Compliance

DATE:	October 24, 2012
TO:	Jeff Klein, MM
FROM:	Bowling Green State University Human Subjects Review Board
PROJECT TITLE:	[338948-4] The Right of Publicity: A Study of the Artist's Negative Voice
SUBMISSION TYPE:	Amendment/Modification
ACTION:	APPROVED
APPROVAL DATE:	October 24, 2012
EXPIRATION DATE:	July 18, 2013
REVIEW TYPE:	Expedited Review
REVIEW CATEGORY:	Expedited review category # 7

Thank you for your submission of Amendment/Modification materials for this project. The Bowling Green State University Human Subjects Review Board has APPROVED your submission. This approval is based on an appropriate risk/benefit ratio and a project design wherein the risks have been minimized. All research must be conducted in accordance with this approved submission.

Modifications Approved:

- Changing the name of the project from "The Right of Publicity: A Study of the Artist's Negative Voice" to "Identity Protection: Copyright, Right of Publicity, and the Artist's Negative Voice." Modified all of the documents containing the original name to reflect the new name and have also changed any applicable descriptions to reflect the new project name.

- Comment: The change of title has been approved. Please go into the Project Overview tab of IRBNet and change your title to "Identity Protection: Copyright, Right of Publicity, and the Artist's Negative Voice".

Please note that you are responsible to conduct the study as approved by the HSRB. If you seek to make any changes in your project activities or procedures, those modifications must be approved by this committee prior to initiation. Please use the modification request form for this procedure.

All UNANTICIPATED PROBLEMS involving risks to subjects or others and SERIOUS and UNEXPECTED adverse events must be reported promptly to this office. All NON-COMPLIANCE issues or COMPLAINTS regarding this project must also be reported promptly to this office.

This approval expires on July 18, 2013. You will receive a continuing review notice before your project expires. If you wish to continue your work after the expiration date, your documentation for continuing review must be received with sufficient time for review and continued approval before the expiration date.

Good luck with your work. If you have any questions, please contact the Office of Research Compliance at 419-372-7716 or hsrb@bgsu.edu. Please include your project title and reference number in all correspondence regarding this project.

Generated on IRBNet

This letter has been electronically signed in accordance with all applicable regulations, and a copy is retained within Bowling Green State University Human Subjects Review Board's records.

www.ingramcontent.com/pod-product-compliance
Lightning Source LLC
Chambersburg PA
CBHW022106170526
45157CB00004B/1507